BARRON'S BOOK NOTES

PEARL BUCK'S

The Good Earth

BARRON'S BOOK NOTES

PEARL BUCK'S
The Good Earth

BY
Ruth Goode

SERIES COORDINATOR
Murray Bromberg
Principal, Wang High School of Queens
Holliswood, New York

BARRON'S EDUCATIONAL SERIES, INC.
Woodbury, New York • London • Toronto • Sydney

ACKNOWLEDGMENTS

Our thanks to Milton Katz and Julius Liebb for their contribution to the Book Notes series.

All inquiries should be addressed to:
Barron's Educational Series, Inc.
113 Crossways Park Drive
Woodbury, New York 11797

Library of Congress Catalog Card No. 85-1362

International Standard Book No. 0-8120-3517-8

Library of Congress Cataloging in Publication Data

Goode, Ruth.
  Pearl Buck's The good earth.

  (Barron's book notes)
  Bibliography: p.104
  Summary: A guide to reading "The Good Earth"
with a critical and appreciative mind.
Includes background on the author's life and
times, sample tests, term paper suggestions,
and a reading list.
  1. Buck, Pearl S. (Pearl Sydenstricker),

1892–1973. Good earth.[1. Buck, Pearl S.
(Pearl Sydenstricker), 1892–1973. Good earth.
2. American literature—History and criticism]
I. Title. II. Series.
PR3503.U198G664   1985   813'.52   85-1362
ISBN 0-8120-3517-8

PRINTED IN THE UNITED STATES OF AMERICA

567   550   987654321

CONTENTS

ADVISORY BOARD

HOW TO USE THIS BOOK

You have to know how to approach literature in order to get the most out of it. This *Barron's Book Notes* volume follows a plan based on methods used by some of the best students to read a work of literature.

Begin with the guide's section on the author's life and times. As you read, try to form a clear picture of the author's personality, circumstances, and motives for writing the work. This background usually will make it easier for you to hear the author's tone of voice, and follow where the author is heading.

Then go over the rest of the introductory material—such sections as those on the plot, characters, setting, themes, and style of the work. Underline, or write down in your notebook, particular things to watch for, such as contrasts between characters and repeated literary devices. At this point, you may want to develop a system of symbols to use in marking your text as you read. (Of course, you should only mark up a book you own, not one that belongs to another person or a school.) Perhaps you will want to use a different letter for each character's name, a different number for each major theme of the book, a different color for each important symbol or literary device. Be prepared to mark up the pages of your book as you read. Put your marks in the margins so you can find them again easily.

Now comes the moment you've been waiting for—the time to start reading the work of literature. You may want to put aside your *Barron's Book Notes* volume until you've read the work all the way through. Or you may want to alternate, reading the *Book Notes* analysis of each section as soon as you have finished reading the corresponding part of the original. Before you move on, reread crucial passages you don't fully understand. (Don't take this guide's analysis for granted—make up your own mind as to what the work means.)

Once you've finished the whole work of literature, you may want to review it right away, so you can firm up your ideas about what it means. You may want to leaf through the book concentrating on passages you marked in reference to one character or one theme. This is also a good time to reread the *Book Notes* introductory material, which pulls together insights on specific topics.

When it comes time to prepare for a test or to write a paper, you'll already have formed ideas about the work. You'll be able to go back through it, refreshing your memory as to the author's exact words and perspective, so that you can support your opinions with evidence drawn straight from the work. Patterns will emerge, and ideas will fall into place; your essay question or term paper will almost write itself. Give yourself a dry run with one of the sample tests in the guide. These tests present both multiple-choice and essay questions. An accompanying section gives answers to the multiple-choice questions as well as suggestions for writing the essays. If you have to select a term paper topic, you may choose one from the list of suggestions in this book. This guide also provides you with a reading list, to help you when you start research for a term paper, and a selection of provocative comments by critics, to spark your thinking before you write.

THE AUTHOR AND HER TIMES

Her house was a mud-walled Chinese farm-house, her neighbors were Chinese farm families, and the only language she heard spoken was the slow, deep-voiced Chinese dialect of the eastern province of Anhwei not far from Shanghai and Nanking. That was where Pearl S. Buck spent the first four years of her marriage to the agricultural specialist John Lossing Buck.

Life in a remote Chinese village was not really strange to Pearl Buck. As the daughter of missionaries, she had lived in China for most of her twenty-five years before her marriage in 1917. Because her father believed in living among the people he preached to, she had grown up and gone to school with Chinese girls, had learned to speak Chinese before she spoke English, and knew Chinese people and their traditional ways at first hand.

What she did not know, and could not have foreseen, was that years later her life among the farm folk of Anhwei would be the source and inspiration of a novel—*The Good Earth*—that would make her world-famous.

Following its publication in 1931, *The Good Earth* led the best-seller lists for some twenty-one months. It won the Pulitzer Prize in 1932 and the William Dean Howells Prize, awarded once in five years by the American Academy of Arts and Letters. It was the work chiefly responsible for her winning the Nobel Prize for Literature in 1938.

Millions of people read *The Good Earth* either in English or in one of the approximately thirty languages—including Chinese—into which it was translated. It was dramatized as a Broadway play (by Owen and Donald Davis) in 1932, and soon afterward it became known to millions more around the world as a motion picture starring Paul Muni, one of the leading actors of the time, in the role of Wang Lung the farmer. The book was hailed not only as a great novel but as a triumph of understanding of Chinese peasant life by a Western woman.

In an extraordinarily productive life of nearly eighty-one years, Pearl Buck wrote novels, short stories, articles, biographies, and an autobiography—in all, more than sixty books. She wrote on American themes as well, but her best creative work drew on her China years. China was her primary home from the age of a few months until 1934, when at forty-two she returned to live permanently in America.

Although Pearl Buck's name in literature is chiefly identified with China, she was born in her grandfather's house in Hillsboro, West Virginia, on June 26, 1892. She was named Pearl by her parents, Absalom and Caroline Sydenstricker, who were Presbyterian missionaries home on leave from China. Pearl was still a baby when the family returned to Chinkiang, near Nanking in the Yangtze River valley. She had a Chinese nurse, and when she reached school age Pearl went to a missionary school for Chinese girls. Her schoolmates called her "Tseng-tzu," Chinese for pearl. She was eight when the Boxer Uprising reached its height in 1900. "Boxer" was the English term for "Fists of Righteous Harmony," the Chinese name of an anti-Western military organization that attacked foreigners and Chinese Christians and endangered the Sydenstricker family. The violence jolted Pearl into realizing for the first time that she was a foreigner.

At seventeen, Pearl made the long journey home and entered Randolph-Macon Woman's College in Lynchburg, Virginia. She spent vacations with her brother and his family, earning pocket money as a tutor to high school students. She loved the lush green woods and fields of the United States and was keenly aware of the healthful conditions of America in contrast with the land where she grew up, but she knew she would go back to China. After graduating in 1914 she stayed on at the college as a teaching assistant in psychology and philosophy, until news that her mother was gravely ill caused her to return to China.

Her mother recovered. In 1917 Pearl married and went to live in the village of Nanhsüchou, in the farming country of northern Anhwei. She worked with her husband among Chinese farmers, and was quickly accepted by them. The deep impression the farmers' lives made on her found its creative outlet in *The Good Earth*, written ten years after she and her husband left Nanhsüchou.

In 1921 the Bucks moved to Nanking, where John joined the university faculty and Pearl taught classes in English literature. Ten years earlier a revolution had ended the Ching, or Manchu, Dynasty and established the Republic of China. Buck had been away at college in the United States at this time. On her return, living first in the provincial city of Chinkiang and then in farm country, she saw little change in the traditional Chinese ways she had known since childhood. In sophisticated Nanking, however, things were different. Nanking had been China's ancient capital, and the revolutionaries had again made it the capital of the Republic. In the city, and especially in the universities, Buck saw a clash of old and new ideas. She wrote articles on the ferment in republican China, and they appeared in such leading American magazines as *The Atlantic Monthly*, *The Nation*, and *The Forum*.

Two shadows darkened these stimulating years. Following surgery in 1919 after the birth of her first child, Buck learned that she could never have another child. Then came the discovery that her daughter Carol was retarded. In 1925 she and her husband took the little girl to the United States for possible treatment, but tests confirmed that the condition was incurable. In *The Good Earth* Pearl Buck may have found some outlet for the emotional strain of these circumstances. Certainly one of the poignant elements in the novel is Wang Lung's fondness for his retarded daughter.

In 1927 civil war broke out between the nationalist and Communist forces that were vying for control in China. The nationalist army attacked Nanking, and Buck and her family, along with other foreigners, were hidden by Chinese friends and evacuated to British and American warships lying offshore. In the turmoil, her manuscript of a completed novel was lost, but her biography of her mother and a portion of a new novel were saved. These tumultuous events, as well as the earlier Boxer Uprising incidents and the civil strife in between, are all reflected in various ways in *The Good Earth*, where they underscore the dissolution of traditional Chinese society and the lack of peace.

Buck's first novel, *East Wind, West Wind*, appeared in 1930, at a time when many publishers believed nobody wanted to read about China. Indeed Buck's publisher, the John Day Publishing Company, later acknowledged that the acceptance of this first novel about the impact of Western ideas on young Chinese was not on its own merit but as an investment in the author's future work.

With the immediate success of *The Good Earth* the publisher's investment paid off. The novel also proved to be a turning point in Buck's life. In 1934 she returned to the United States for good. After divorcing John Buck she married Richard J. Walsh, president of the John Day Company. She and her second husband moved into a stone farmhouse in Pennsylvania, and over the next several years they adopted five children, two boys and three girls.

Buck continued the epic of the Wang family with two sequels to *The Good Earth*: *Sons* (1932) and *A House Divided* (1935); together they formed a trilogy called *The House of Earth*. There followed a steady stream of novels, short stories, and children's books with American as well as Chinese backgrounds. Interspersed with these were memoirs, articles for popular magazines, and biographies of her mother (*The Exile*) and father (*Fighting Angel*).

Buck was enormously popular as a personality, constantly in demand for lectures on writing, on adoption, on mental retardation, and on American involvement in the Far East. But none of these other activities stemmed the flow of her fiction. When her rate of production outran her publisher's ability to market her novels, she used the pen name "John Sedges." Five of her books appeared under this name, beginning with *The Townsman*, an American historical novel (1945).

Although critics found few of her novels equal to *The Good Earth*, her gifts as a storyteller won her a worldwide readership. She became one of the most widely translated U.S. authors.

Pearl Buck's contribution to American understanding of China and the Far East in general was matched by her dedication to human rights and racial equality, and to the rescue of children of American soldiers serving in the Far East and Asian women (such children often were shunned in Asian society). She founded Welcome House, an adoption agency to find such children of mixed ancestry American homes, and the Pearl S. Buck Foundation, to help them in their own countries.

Pearl Buck died in 1973, three months short of her eighty-first birthday. People who paid tribute agreed that Buck had made a great contribution to Western understanding of China, especially in *The Good Earth*. By the time you have finished reading the novel, you too will have learned a lot about China and the Chinese people as well as about people in general.

THE NOVEL

The Plot

Wang Lung is a young farmer, living with his aged father in a tiny three-room house outside a country town in northern China. Since his mother's death six years earlier, Wang has done all the housework, cared for his father, and worked in his fields. The novel opens on the day he brings home the wife his father has bought for him, O-lan, a young slave woman from the great House of Hwang.

After their first son's birth, Wang buys a piece of land for growing rice from the Hwang estate. For a while he prospers, but a long drought causes his crops to fail, and Wang and his family, along with their neighbors, begin to starve. O-lan endures another pregnancy during this famine, but she kills the newborn daughter that she cannot feed. They are forced to sell their furniture, but they will not part with their land. With the two pieces of silver the furniture brings them, Wang Lung and O-lan, with Wang's aged father and their three young children, climb aboard a train carrying the stream of refugees to the city, one hundred miles to the south.

Away from his land and no longer a farmer, Wang is lost. He tries to maintain his dignity by refusing to beg, but his poorly paid efforts as an honest laborer cannot feed the family. Only the begging of O-lan and the children provides some relief.

One day Wang is swept along with a mob that

breaks into a rich man's house. He suddenly comes face to face with the terrified owner, and when the man offers Wang money to spare his life, Wang takes everything the man has. He takes his family home and spends his sudden wealth on a good ox, new farm implements, and the best-quality seeds. O-lan also has been involved in the recent plunder and has brought back a treasure of jewels. Wang takes from her all but two little pearls that she asks to keep. With this treasure he buys the rest of the land from the now destitute House of Hwang.

Wang Lung is a rich man, with stores of grain and rice as protection against future famine. He takes in his good neighbor Ching, who lost his wife and daughter in the famine, to help in working the new land.

Meanwhile O-lan has borne twins, a boy and a girl. Wang has much business to conduct in selling his crops. Because he has never learned to read and write, he is embarrassed by his inability to read a contract. Thus he sends his two older sons to school in the town.

When a flood covers the land for months, preventing farming, Wang in restless idleness visits the new tea house, a house of prostitution in the town. He becomes infatuated with Lotus Flower, a dainty and sophisticated prostitute, and showers her with gifts.

Then Wang's uncle, a man of bad character and reputation, arrives with his wife and son. Because of the customs governing blood relationships, Wang cannot refuse to take them in. The uncle's wife, a worldly woman, arranges Wang's purchase of Lotus as his concubine, a secondary wife and mistress. Wang adds quarters to the house for Lotus and her servant, the one-time slave Cuckoo.

Wang's first daughter, who suffered starvation as an infant during the famine, has proved to be retarded. Wang is devoted to his "poor fool," and he becomes angry with Lotus for the first time when he finds her screaming at the child. He is even more enraged when he finds his eldest son spending time with Lotus, and he beats them both.

Wang Lung has betrothed his eldest son to a daughter of the grain merchant Liu, and his youngest daughter to Liu's son. He has placed his second son, a shrewd lad with a head for trade, as an apprentice in Liu's business. He intends his third son to become a farmer like himself. After arranging his children's futures to his satisfaction, Wang suddenly realizes that silent, uncomplaining O-lan is very ill and close to death.

After the birth of the twins, O-lan had spoken once of having "a fire in her vitals." Wang realizes for the first time how much he owes to her. O-lan asks only to see her eldest son married before she dies. Wang arranges a fine wedding feast for the boy and his bride, and O-lan dies contented. Soon after, Wang's aged father dies.

Although Wang's uncle's son has run off to become a soldier, the uncle and his wife remain. They contribute nothing, but they expect to be served expensive food and drink, and they also demand money. Because his uncle is secretly a member of the notorious Redbeards, a gang of robbers, Wang must keep these parasites to protect his house and family from the robber gang. The eldest son cunningly suggests that Wang supply his uncle and aunt with opium. Perhaps he can make them harmless, dreaming addicts. He also proposes that Wang leave them in the old farmhouse and move his own family to the Hwang mansion in the town, which is for rent. As Wang's fortunes have risen, the fortunes of the once intimidating Hwang house have declined. Wang accepts both of his son's suggestions.

Wang's eldest son and his wife present Wang with his first grandchild, a boy. The miserly second son is also married. Wang has found for him, as he asked, not a delicately bred city girl like his brother's wife, but a robust village girl of simpler (inexpensive) tastes. Wang makes this money-minded son the steward of his now considerable estate. In due time Wang has seven grandchildren, with whom he spends his happiest hours.

Into this peaceful home one day bursts a band of soldiers, led by the late uncle's dissolute son, who eat and carouse at Wang Lung's expense. They stay for weeks, wrecking the fine furniture and gardens and menacing the females of the household, who must be kept in seclusion.

Wang's peace is also disturbed by the bickering of his sons' wives. He is troubled by his youngest son, who has no taste for farming but wants to become a soldier. The youth is attracted to Pear Blossom, a delicate young slave girl in Lotus' service. When he finds that his father, Wang, wants this girl for himself, the youth storms out of the house. Later Wang learns that this third son has become a high-ranking officer in the south.

Pear Blossom becomes the love of Wang's old age. Feeling his years, he moves with her, his "poor fool," and a few servants, back to the old farmhouse where he can be near his land again. When he hears his two sons talking about selling the land, he cries out against such a plan. They reassure him, but over the old man's head they smile at one another.

The Characters

MAJOR CHARACTERS

Wang Lung

This simple, hard-working Chinese farmer is the central figure in *The Good Earth*. This is his story, and it is told largely through his eyes. Some readers feel that he is not just a Chinese peasant but a universal one, an example of people who have tilled the earth throughout the ages.

You may not agree with the description of Wang Lung as the universal farmer, if this seems to make him no more than a symbol. To be sure, people have lived and toiled like Wang in many lands, whether in Asia or Africa, Europe of the Middle Ages or colonial America. Many, in fact, still do. But you can also say that Wang Lung is not just a representative peasant but an individual human being who is warm, believable, and sympathetic. As a human he also has his flaws.

Some readers point out that Wang is quick to anger and often acts on impulse. He cares too much about public opinion and what people will think of him, so he often gives in to situations too easily. Many times his wife O-lan provides him with strength and decisiveness. One example of his softness during a critical situation is his inability to kill the ox that has shared his hours of toil, even though his children are starving.

But Wang's tender heart also has a positive side. He can be as tender with people as he is with animals. He cannot bear to sell his daughter during the famine, although Chinese fathers have followed such a custom for centuries. He is reluctant to give the weeping slave girl, Pear Blossom, to his brutal soldier cousin who terrifies her. His affection for his honest neighbor Ching is so deep that he is ready to bury the man in the family plot and is stopped only by his sons' outraged protests.

You may feel that Wang's greatest failure is his treatment of his wife O-lan. Wang himself realizes this on occasion, and he is ashamed. Yet Wang has genuine moments of tenderness toward O-lan. When he brings her home for the first time, he takes her heavy box and carries it himself, an unusual act for a Chinese husband. After their wedding night he is anxious to know whether she is as pleased with him as he is with her. And several times, when she shows herself to be wise as well as strong and capable, he takes pride in her and congratulates himself on having such a woman, although it never occurs to him to tell her so.

In taking O-lan for granted, Wang may exhibit a common human flaw. But isn't his treatment of his wife also related to the inferior status of women in Chinese tradition? Wang acquires a wife in the first place not by his own choice but by his father's. Her most important function is to bear him sons. The taking of a concubine or second wife for pleasure was an accepted practice. Is he obliged to love O-lan or be loyal to her? There's no simple explanation of this relationship, and readers differ in their opinions about it.

Other traditions govern Wang Lung's behavior.

One you will find to be significant is the ancient rule of respect for elders and relatives. Besides causing his concern for the community's favorable opinion, this rule obliges Wang to accept his uncle and the uncle's family even though they are free-loaders who take all they can from him.

Wang has his own strict ideas of right and wrong. When he and his family become refugees in the southern city, he refuses to beg. Instead he pulls a riksha, a two-wheeled cart, even though he takes in less money at this gruelling work than O-lan and the children with their begging. When his second son steals a piece of meat, Wang plucks it out of the stew, throws it on the ground, and later beats the boy in punishment.

Wang is human, so don't be surprised to find him inconsistent. Given the chance and pressed by poverty, he extorts money from the frightened rich man by threatening the man's life, and he accepts the jewels that O-lan has stolen in the same raid. But he feels no guilt about this illicit wealth because he uses it to save his land and buy more. The land is his anchor, and away from it he loses direction.

You may feel there is another inconsistency in the simple farmer—his weakness for female beauty. Although he knows that bound feet, traditional objects of beauty, would be of no value to a poor farmer, he is disappointed that O-lan has big feet. (Women with bound feet—feet kept small and re-shaped by binding at a young age—find it very painful to walk long distances or to carry heavy loads.) He also notes her plain face with some dis-taste. This longing for feminine beauty makes Wang a too-willing victim of the practiced wiles of Lotus

Flower. Yet again, you may want to ask how much of this is Wang's personal failure and how much that of his culture.

As he grows older, Wang longs for peace in his house. But his sons argue, his daughters-in-law bicker, and he finds peace only on his land. His passion for the land overrides all other emotions. The land is his livelihood, his security, and the source from which he draws spiritual refreshment. In the face of starvation he will not sell a single field. The last words we hear from him as an old man are his appeal to his sons, "If you will sell the land, it is the end."

O-lan

Some readers have found O-lan the most appealing character in the novel. She reveals very little about herself in words, but you will find out a good deal about her thoughts and feelings from her actions. She was sold by her poor parents to the great Hwang household at the age of ten, during a famine. Too plain to be desirable as a concubine, she was a good worker and so was kept as a kitchen slave. When she is twenty years old, tall, and strongly built she is sold to be Wang Lung's wife.

Note her behavior in her new role as wife. She cooks the wedding feast, but she declines to show herself to Wang's male guests: she is modest and knows the proprieties. She is quick and thorough in performing her household duties, so that she has time to do more than is expected of her. She works beside Wang at hoeing and planting, and yet has his meal on the table when he comes in from his work.

What does this say about O-lan? Perhaps she is happier now than she has ever been since her childhood. You might say that she has achieved what she never dared hope for in her years as a kitchen slave. She is mistress of her own household. She has a husband who does not beat her or order her about but is on the whole gentle and considerate in the small, everyday ways that sweeten life.

O-lan does not express her happiness in words. But it may be revealed in her pride in her household, the care she takes to mend and repair Wang's meager possessions, her diligence, and her thrift. Could you interpret this as evidence that O-lan sees herself as sharing in a joint enterprise with her husband, not as a slave wife but as a co-worker? Might this explain why she persists in working in the fields throughout her pregnancy, right up to the onset of her labor pains, and then returns to the fields again with scarcely any rest after giving birth? Possibly you feel O-lan is sometimes extreme in her stoicism and doesn't do enough to make her life easier.

Although she is slow in her speech, O-lan is not slow-witted. She's alert to everything that is going on around her. She recognizes the first signs of decline in the House of Hwang and sets Wang on his land-buying course. Her resourcefulness is largely responsible for the family's surviving the famine, from the sale of the furniture that provides money to take them south, to the hoard of jewels that she steals in the city.

When Wang brings Lotus into the house, O-lan knows she has no choice by tradition but to outwardly accept her husband's concubine. She breaks her stoic silence, though, to reveal her depth of feeling when she responds to a rebuke from Wang, "To that one you gave my two pearls."

O-lan's illness begins after the birth of twins, but she still goes about her work without complaint until even Wang realizes how ill she is. Through the long winter he sits beside her as she waits for death. When he exclaims that he would sell all his land if it would heal her, she answers that she would not let him, since she must die anyway,"but the land is there after me."

OTHER CHARACTERS

The other characters in *The Good Earth* are not as fully developed as Wang Lung and O-lan. They are often types that reflect various aspects of Chinese society. But they also contribute to the progress of the story, and each one reveals some facet of Wang Lung's personality and of the picture of life in China. Some of these characters have no names but are identified only by their relationship to Wang Lung. In Chinese families, one is usually identified by a relationship rather than a proper name.

Wang Lung's Father

This once hard-working farmer is a frail old man who demands the care and respect that are due him in his old age. He complains when his comfort is not properly attended to, and he scolds Wang Lung for spending money to celebrate his wedding or the birth of a son. At the same time he is proud that his son can make such a fine show before the neighbors. As the story of Wang progresses, you will notice certain traits shared by father and son. What are they? How do the men differ?

The old man has absolute faith that his son and grandsons will take care of him, and he endures the hardships of the famine with good nature. He has an earthy sense of humor. When O-lan gives birth to twins, for example, he exclaims, "An egg with a double yolk this time!" He is also capable of simple loyalty to the past. When he sees Lotus, the concubine, painted and dressed in silks, he refuses to accept her, insisting that one wife was enough for him and for his father before him. Wang's father illustrates the old-fashioned virtues and especially the virtue of deference to one's parents and ancestors.

Wang Lung's Uncle

Unlike Wang's father and Wang himself, this younger brother of the old man is a shiftless farmer who is careless of his house and land and lets his children run wild in the town. He exploits the traditional obligation toward blood relatives to prey upon Wang. During the famine he sells his eldest daughter and his younger children disappear without explanation. He and his wife and son continue to be well-fed and are even suspected of cannibalism. A gambler at the beginning of the story, he later turns out to have criminal connections. He seems to represent the disintegration of life and family that follows breaking with the land. If you agree that he is the nastiest character in the book, do you think Wang Lung should have dealt with him differently, given Chinese family obligations?

The Uncle's Wife

This fat, self-indulgent woman takes full advantage of her husband's hold over Wang Lung. She demands delicacies of food and drink, and she does no work in the household. But neither does she do any real mischief. On the contrary, she is useful to Wang in arranging the purchase of Lotus. Her gossipy good humor pleases Lotus, but their closeness bothers Wang.

The Uncle's Son

As a youthful scamp, he has a bad influence in Wang's house. He has no respect for family or tradition and introduces Wang's eldest son to drinking and seeing prostitutes. He also tries to seduce Wang's younger daughter before going off to fight in the local civil warfare. He returns when Wang is rich and has moved into the Great House. Although he has become a coarse and brutal ruffian, he has some of the sinister charm of an adventurer. He leaves one of Wang's household slaves pregnant as he goes off, laughing and without a care. An echo of his influence comes later, when Wang's third son storms out of the house to follow in his soldier cousin's footsteps.

Wang Lung's Eldest Son

When Wang Lung begins to prosper, he gives his first-born son an education and arranges his marriage to a girl of the middle class, the daughter of a grain merchant. Unlike Wang, the son grows up contemptuous of the land. While his father wants only to be a wealthy farmer, this son aspires to go beyond the family's farm origins and live in the style of the young lords of the House of Hwang. He is the one who persuades Wang to move into the mansion in the town, which he furnishes and decorates in aristocratic style. In Wang's old age you see this son already plotting with his brother to divide and sell the land. Some readers see in this son a symbol of the old Chinese aristocracy with all its pompousness.

Wang Lung's Second Son

To Wang's distress, this son is also unwilling to work in the fields but demands an education like his brother. He is quick and shrewd, and he progresses from an apprenticeship in the grain merchant's business to becoming Wang's steward over the growing estate. In contrast to his elder brother, he loves money not for what it can buy but for itself. He wants a wife who will not ask for expensive luxuries like his brother's, and he stints even on his wedding feast. His tight control of their father's money irks his elder brother, so that these two have a running feud. They agree, however, on the project of selling the land after their father's death. You might see in this son another facet of traditional Chinese society, the landless merchant class that made its money by squeezing the poor.

Wang Lung's Daughters-in-Law

The wives of Wang's first and second sons rarely appear directly in the story but the contrast in their two characters is striking. The eldest son's wife, proper and conventional, urges her husband on in his aspiration toward upper-class status. The second son's bride is a hearty, robust village girl with a lively, unconventional style. The two women bicker constantly, sharpening the underlying feud between their husbands and depriving the household of the peace that Wang Lung longs for.

Wang Lung's Third Son

The youngest of Wang's sons, one of twins, disappoints Wang's hope of raising one son who will love and work the land. This son, too, demands an education. A silent boy, he keeps his thoughts and wishes to himself. From his cousin and the soldiers quartered in the house, he gains a taste for soldiering, and he runs away to join one of the armies roaming the region. When last heard of, he has become a high-ranking revolutionary officer. Some readers see in this son the new China which has lost all contact with the land and tradition.

Wang Lung's Elder Daughter

O-lan's third child, she was born just before the famine. The deprivations of her first years have left her retarded. Wang makes her his special care. He feels a profound tenderness for his "poor fool," as he calls her, and is anxious about how she will fare after he dies, until his last love, the concubine Pear Blossom, promises to care for her. You might argue that Wang's "poor fool" represents all those who have suffered from starvation and poverty. She also reflects a good side of Wang.

Wang Lung's Younger Daughter

The third son's girl twin turns out to be a pretty child, and Wang arranges a marriage for her to one of the grain merchant's sons. In preparation for the little girl's future in a middle-class family, O-lan binds her feet. When Wang discovers her weeping over the pain and offers to have her feet unbound, this daughter refuses, saying that then her husband will not love her. Wang's younger daughter illustrates the fate of a girl in a well-to-do Chinese family. Following custom, she leaves her parents' home forever to join her husband's family and come under the rule of her mother-in-law. How do you think this would be received by the young married women you know?

Lotus Flower

Lotus Flower is a high-class prostitute. She is painted, perfumed, dressed in silks and jewels, skilled in pleasing men and exacting expensive gifts from them. She can scarcely walk on her tiny bound feet and is not expected to do any work in the house where she comes to live as Wang's concubine. Selfish and self-indulgent, Lotus Flower exerts considerable power over Wang until her behavior toward his children offends him, and he frees himself from his emotional dependence on her. Although a slave, as his concubine she has a secure and permanent place in the household, and as Wang grows old she simply grows fatter, lazier, and more self-indulgent. Before condemning Lotus Flower, though, consider what options she had, or perhaps didn't have, as a girl sold into slavery.

Cuckoo

Cuckoo was the Old Lord's last slave in the House of Hwang before its downfall. She later becomes the proprietor of the house of prostitution where Wang finds Lotus, and she comes into Wang's household as Lotus' servant. A shrewd, sharp-tongued woman, she appears cunning and grasping. Might you find a more sympathetic interpretation of her character as a woman who has spent her entire life in slavery and is seeking only security in her later years? In Wang's household she is at last secure for the rest of her life.

Pear Blossom

Wang buys this small, frail seven-year-old girl as a little serving maid for Lotus. She grows into a pretty young woman who catches the eye first of Wang's soldier cousin and then of Wang's youngest son. When Wang is attracted to her himself, she convinces him that she likes only old men because they are kind. You might consider whether, unlike the more robust Cuckoo, Pear Blossom has responded to a life in slavery by becoming more sensitive to the unfortunate and rejected. She becomes Wang's mistress and a comfort in his later years when he is rejected by his own family, and she volunteers to take care of Wang's retarded daughter after his death.

Ching

From the beginning, Wang feels a brotherly affection for this honest neighbor, a poor farmer like himself, described in the novel as a "small, spare, lean man of great gravity." In the worst days of the famine, Ching proves his friendship by sharing his last remaining food, a handful of dried beans, with Wang for the pregnant O-lan. When Wang comes back from the south with his new wealth, Ching is barely alive. As Wang's partner and later his overseer, he proves himself a capable farm manager worthy of Wang's trust. When Ching dies, Wang feels that he has lost his only true friend. Besides O-lan, he is the only character who remains consistently true to the "good earth."

The Old Lord and the Old Mistress

The Old Lord, head of the House of Hwang, and the Old Mistress, his first wife and matriarch of the household, are an intimidating pair to Wang at the beginning of the story. But the Hwang fortunes are already fading. The five young lords (sons) are away in the city, spending their wealth on pleasures. The Old Lord is occupied with his concubines, the Old Mistress with her opium, and nobody cares for the land. These two characters and the House of Hwang present an object lesson in the rise and fall of families. Wang Lung's family seems destined for the same end.

Other Elements

SETTING

Wang Lung's inherited strip of farmland is in the northerly part of the province of Anhwei, a cold, dry country. Once every five years or so it suffers a drought in which no crops grow. The region is bare of forests, so there is no wood for building or for fuel. With no woodlands to hold back the run-off of rains, there is also flooding. A third hazard is a periodic plague of locusts that devour the crops when they are close to harvest. In *The Good Earth*, Wang and his neighbors are visited by all three of these disasters in succession.

Wang's house and land lie outside the walled country town. His house has three tiny rooms, a thatched roof, and walls made of earthen bricks, with small window holes covered over with paper to keep out the winter cold. The kitchen is nothing but an earthen oven in a shed shared with the ox's stall. The cooking fire in the oven consists of a handful of straw and dried grass, and Wang lights it with a spark struck from a flint chip with a scrap of iron. Although the end of Wang's story takes place in the late 1920s, Chinese farmers have lived this way for many hundreds of years.

With his growing prosperity, Wang's little house is enlarged in the style of Chinese dwellings: additional rooms are built around an open court. Later, when the setting changes to the House of Hwang within the town, you see an elegant Chinese mansion, with carved furniture and screens, courtyard after courtyard planted with flowering trees, and a goldfish or lily pool in its center.

When Wang takes his starving family south during the famine, the setting shifts to a city, probably Chinkiang, in the coastal province of Kiangsu. Here the climate is mild, and the outlying farms grow a great variety of crops, which are harvested twice a year. Farmers also use "night soil" (that is, human excrement) to fertilize their fields. It is a rich city, thriving with trade and tea houses where businessmen gamble and take their pleasures, and the markets are plentiful enough to feed all the starving in Anhwei, could the food be transported.

Historically, China had no distribution system that could relieve famine in one region with food from another. Even under the republic founded in 1911, there was no strong central government to carry out such a rescue. Whole provinces were ruled not by the government in Nanking, but by local leaders with their own armies, called "war lords." Pearl Buck does not give you exact dates for her story, but from the echo of events that takes place outside Wang's narrow world, it probably covers the period from 1890 through the late 1920s.

THEMES

1. THE EARTH

The main theme of *The Good Earth* is announced in its title: it is the good earth itself. The story follows Wang Lung's climb from poverty to riches, from toiling peasant to wealthy landowner. But all along the way—like signposts on a road—you may read messages pointing to the deeper meaning of the story, the life-sustaining bond of human beings with the land. Wang always returns to this.

Wang receives his livelihood and spiritual rejuvenation from the land. He experiences harmony with O-lan working beside him. His sole source of stability is in the land, and this is why he always transforms any material gain into land. You see the decline of the House of Hwang as it becomes separated from the land, and the same seems to hold for Wang when he is apart from his land.

What do you make of the turn in the story by which Wang Lung's fortunes rise—not from the fruit of the earth but from the money and jewels he and O-lan have stolen? Is it possible that the author means that labor and the good earth are not enough? That the poor farmer couldn't survive without a stroke of good fortune or the opportunity to take something from the rich? Or, perhaps this money is the evil seed of the Wang family's eventual disintegration. Frequently in the book, silver and land are presented as opposing values, as when O-lan takes silver for the furniture but won't sell the land before leaving for the south.

2. THE STATUS OF WOMEN

Pearl Buck uses the inferior status of women in traditional China with great emotional impact. The casual way in which a fellow refugee talks of strangling a girl child at birth or selling her as a slave is in itself a shock. Wang Lung and O-lan deal with both these alternatives. A crucial event in their marital relationship occurs when O-lan, submitting as she must to her husband's authority, hands over her two small pearls. Although women's roles varied, all were subservient. As a peasant wife a woman worked both in the house and in the fields. She could be a household slave, like Cuckoo. She could be a prostitute serving any man's pleasure in a tea house, like Lotus Flower, or a concubine serving only her master's pleasure, again like Lotus when she assumes this role in Wang's house. Finally, she could be an upper-class wife like the eldest son's wife in the Great House, with servants to wait on her and do the housework. Rich or poor, if she is a wife, her principal function is to bear sons.

Another aspect of Chinese life that seemed designed to make women suffer was the practice of altering the feet of girls so they could barely walk. The Chinese custom of foot-binding was meant to please men esthetically and to enhance a man's status by showing he was wealthy enough for his wife or concubine not to work. You might compare bound feet with the "wasp" waists that were fashionable for Western women in the nineteenth century. Those waists, which a man could encircle with his two hands, were achieved only by tight corseting that forced the internal organs out of place and often caused injury. Tight corseting was not as crippling as foot-binding but it had the same purpose—to please men.

3. THE FAMILY
The family is historically the central unit of Chinese society. In *The Good Earth* it is also the center of Wang Lung's world, second only to his attachment to the land. Precise rules govern all relationships in the Chinese family. A member's position in the family determines his behavior and even his name. You see this in the novel, in which Wang Lung's sons are spoken of as Eldest Son or Second Son, and the uncle's family are not aunt or cousin but the uncle's wife and the uncle's son. The rules are binding: a wife is obedient to her husband and children to their father, and everyone—husbands, wives, children—must respect the elderly.

The dominance of males runs through these rules as well. A wife who has borne sons, like O-lan, is entitled to more respect and consideration from her husband than if she has borne only daughters. Wang Lung is obliged to yield to the demands of his uncle and the uncle's family because they are related to him on his father's side.

You may find this particular obligation unfair, imposing a heavy burden on Wang Lung, especially considering the character of the uncle and his family. Wang frees himself from their demands only by supplying his uncle and aunt with opium, an addictive and debilitating drug.

On the other hand, Wang's father is so sure that

his son and grandsons will look after him that he endures the hardships of the famine with smiling good humor. His trust is well founded. Wang Lung gives him the first share of whatever food there is, even if he must deprive his own children. Some nomadic societies leave the old people who cannot keep up with the migration to starve and die. Can you make a case for either of these two customs? Are both too extreme?

Wang Lung gives his old father not only respect and obedience but also loving care. From his own sons Wang receives only a show of respect. As you read, consider why Wang Lung fails so completely to understand his sons. Is this simply a case of the generation gap? You may want to remember that Wang grew up as the hard-working son of a poor farmer, while they grew up as sons of a prosperous landowner.

4. RELIGION AND GOOD FORTUNE

Wang Lung's religious beliefs are a mixture of different traditions. Primarily, since he is a farmer, he worships (burns incense) before two small earth gods in the field to bring good fortune to himself and his family. But he also appeals to the goddess of mercy to give his daughter-in-law a boy child in return for a new robe. He buys a paper god of wealth when his fortunes are on the rise and scolds the gods when misfortune occurs. He is superstitious and believes in omens. He tries to fool the evil spirits, as when he hides his own baby boy under his robe and proclaims out loud that it is only a worthless girl child.

Wang Lung also respects the more sophisticated

Confucian principles of family deference and is pleased when his son erects an ancestral shrine in the house. As a matter of convention he gives donations to both the Buddhist and Taoist temples on the birth of his first son. This mixture of deference to the ancient philosophies and to the spirit world was typical of everyday Chinese religious practice. However, the more established religious institutions seem more the preserve of the educated. For a simple farmer like Wang, even when he becomes rich, the little earthen idols—gods of the renewal of life—are supremely powerful. Although he treats them badly and blames them for misfortune, he is afraid to reject them totally, and he ultimately returns to them since they have "power over earth."

Wang's personal conversations with his gods may seem a bit disrespectful to you. But if you believed, as Wang did, that these gods had purposely created your good fortune or your bad times, you might respond in the same way. How does your religious heritage teach you to deal with adversity?

5. MORALITY AND NECESSITY

You may agree that on the whole Wang Lung is a good man. O-lan, too, strikes most readers as a genuinely good woman. But there are certainly grounds to argue the contrary, at least on some issues. Infanticide, pillaging, slavery, drug selling, and other less severe actions raise questions about what codes of morality do exist in the novel. Western readers have to keep in mind differences between their culture and that of Wang Lung, where custom allows some unfamiliar behavior. You might ask, however, whether custom and morality, a sense of right and wrong, are the same thing. Or is there a morality so basic to human beings that local customs, though widely accepted, are actually violations of that morality?

In a world as harsh as Wang Lung's, morality may not always be so clear. As Wang and the other Chinese struggle to survive, what role does necessity play? Is there a justification for stealing? For infanticide? Under what circumstances?

6. WANG LUNG'S SEARCH FOR PEACE

As he prospers and his life becomes complicated with family relationships, Wang Lung increasingly longs for peace in his household but never finds it. O-lan does not create the trouble he expected over Lotus Flower, but she makes difficulties with Lotus' servant Cuckoo. Wang fails entirely to understand his sons. All three of them disappoint him by rejecting the land. For a time Wang finds peace in watching his grandchildren at play, but when they are of school age they giggle at his old-fashioned ideas and he stops visiting them. Only the land has given him the peace he seeks, and so in old age he moves from the mansion in the town back to the old farmhouse, where he can spend his last years in peace, close to his fields.

This lack of domestic tranquility is reflected in the wars and civil strife that surround the personal story of Wang Lung. The turmoil of a society in transition from an imperial autocracy to a modern republic intrudes periodically in the form of soldiers, looters, rioters, and bandits. The uncle's family—with a bandit father and a dissolute soldier son—is another example of the uprooted, warlike events that disturb the peace of Wang and his family.

STYLE

Much has been written about Pearl Buck's style of writing in *The Good Earth*. One critic calls it "almost Biblical," while others compare it to ancient folk epics. Another critic describes it as a mixture of the King James Version of the Bible and a traditional Chinese epic.

A writer's style can't always be traced to the influences of his or her childhood reading, but in Pearl Buck's case the two influences mentioned above did exist. As the daughter of Presbyterian missionaries, Buck was brought up on the Bible. And although she read widely in English literature, she also read Chinese novels.

As Buck herself explained, Chinese novels were written for a wide popular audience. They developed from the tales that professional storytellers once told to a crowd of people sitting on the ground around them, at a time when most Chinese—like most people everywhere—could neither read nor write. Buck translated one of these Chinese novels into English, and she lectured and wrote on the popular art of the Chinese novel.

Buck wrote *The Good Earth* at great speed, finishing it in three months. It was as though the story and all its characters had been growing in her mind like seeds in the earth, until the right moment came for them to blossom in the pages of her novel.

Buck's writing style reflects this swift stream of inspiration. There is nothing forced or difficult about her style. Her sentences and paragraphs flow clearly and easily, without effort. She tells us Wang Lung's thoughts and feelings in the simple words in which a farmer who could not read or write might think and feel them.

Because her characters are not given to much talk, she does not use much dialogue. When they do talk, their turns of phrase seem to suggest that they are talking in their native language. Yet every word and every sentence they utter is good, simple English.

Try reading aloud some passages of dialogue from the novel. See if you can tell what makes them sound as though they might be speaking Chinese. Is it perhaps the rhythm, rather than the words? Buck once said that she thought out all her stories in Chinese first, before writing them down in English.

POINT OF VIEW

The Good Earth is a third-person narrative, but the story it tells is Wang Lung's. Everything that happens is described as he experiences it and as it affects him. The narrator explains Wang Lung's thoughts and feelings but almost never those of other characters. You understand them through their words and actions.

This is obviously a rather limiting way of telling a story. In staying strictly within Wang Lung's experience, the narrator can't be all-knowing. You might think that the novel could have been written in the first person, with Wang Lung as the "I." But this hero is an uneducated, indeed an illiterate farmer, and if the story were told in his words the

novel would be limited not only to his experiences
but to his vocabulary. In using the third-person
form the narrator has somewhat more scope.

Yet the scope is quite limited. For example, when
O-lan brings a bowl of tea to her husband on the
first morning of their marriage, you know that she
is afraid of him only because he sees the fear in
her expression. Later you see that O-lan comes to
trust her husband from the way that she goes about
her work, taking her full share of the toil as an
equal partner, and also from the way she offers
advice to Wang Lung on the rare occasions when
a crisis moves her to break her customary silence.

Just as the characters are described only as they
affect Wang Lung, every event is told only as it
relates to him. Drought, flood, locusts—all are part
of the story only as they affect Wang Lung. Wars
are fought all over China and robber bands plunder and murder in the villages, but we learn of
these dire events only as Wang Lung does. His
uncle turns out to be a member of a notorious band
of brigands. He learns that a robber band raided
the House of Hwang during the famine. His cousin
brings a band of soldiers into his house. He learns
that his third son has become a high official in the
"revolution."

The narrator does not explain aspects of Chinese
life that would be outside of Wang Lung's knowl-
edge or comprehension, even though they might
be interesting to a European or American reader.
The novel pursues an unswerving story line, faith-
fully following the experience of the central character. Wouldn't you think that this would be too
narrow a point of view to be interesting? Would

you expect one simple Chinese peasant's life in a remote country village to make an absorbing, suspenseful story?

FORM AND STRUCTURE

The Good Earth is a novel in the form of a biography. The story is told chronologically from the hero's young manhood to his old age, a period covering roughly forty years.

The novel is made up of thirty-four chapters and falls into two main parts. The first fourteen chapters establish Wang Lung's commitment to the land and depict his solid family relationships with his wife and father. His achievement of modest prosperity is followed by a sudden reversal in the form of poverty and famine which drives him and his family to the city to beg and perform hired labor. Chapters 11 to 14, which take place in the city, provide a striking contrast to the earlier depiction of country life and its traditional values. The climax of the first part of the book occurs in Chapter 14 when city unrest leads Wang and his wife, O-lan, to join a raid on a rich man's house. The money and jewels they steal enable them to return to the land. The illegal gain proves the turning point of Wang's life and fortune.

The second part of *The Good Earth* follows Wang's fortunes from his return to his village, through his acquisition of more and more land (Chapters 15 to 19), to his eventual acquisition of the mansion of the former grand family of the district, the Hwangs (Chapters 26 to 29). His rise in wealth and status is accompanied by his fall from a state of contentment as he alienates himself from the land and his family. The last five chapters reveal the price Wang pays for his wealth. He is alone; his wife is dead and so is his father. His sons are unsympathetic to traditional ways and to the land, and even his grandchildren laugh at him for his old-fashioned ways. He moves back to his farmhouse with a young slave girl who acts as a daughter and with his own mentally retarded daughter whom nobody else would care for.

The Story

CHAPTER 1

It is Wang Lung's wedding day. He rises at dawn as always to light the fire and heat the water, but today is different. Instead of merely washing, he fills the wooden tub and bathes. He puts aside his padded winter suit, now torn and soiled, for a clean one of cotton, and over it goes his one cotton coat saved for feast days. He brushes out and rebraids his queue, the traditional long lock of hair growing from the crown of his head, and he weaves a tasseled black silk cord into the braid.

His old father complains: such wastefulness! Water for a bath, tea leaves in the bowl of hot water Wang brings him: "It is the day," says Wang.

In the town, Wang has the barber shave his head around the queue but balks at cutting off the queue, as is now the fashion: for that he must ask his father's permission. In the market he buys a little pork, a little beef, and a small fish for his wedding feast. At last everything is done, and he must now go to the great House of Hwang, the residence of the district's biggest landowner, and fetch his bride, a young slave woman his father has bought for him and whom he has never seen.

At the gate of the mansion he stops, faint with nervousness: he forgot to eat this morning. Back into the town he goes, to gulp tea and noodles in the tea house, dawdling so long that he is asked to pay extra. He jumps up and heads for the great house again. Here the gateman treats him with scorn, demands a tip, and finally ushers him into the presence of the Old Mistress. The tiny, withered old lady summons O-lan.

In little more than a dozen pages you have a graphic image of the little farmhouse, the frugal way of life, the demanding old father, and the novel's hero. Wang Lung is a farmer. He is young, shy, practically a stranger in his own village where he rarely goes, having no money to spend. He is intimidated even by the tea house boy, let alone the arrogant gateman, and all but falls on his face before the Old Mistress. Does this introduction to the central character strike you as having a particular blend of comedy and pathos like that of Charlie Chaplin movies? From here on the mood changes, and comedy gives way to deeper levels of sympathy. Watch especially how O-lan's character emerges, how she is described only by her actions and the way Wang sees her, and how you can gather clues about what she thinks and feels. This is a good example of Pearl Buck's skill at characterization.

O-lan appears. The Old Mistress tells Wang about her—"She is not beautiful, but that you do not need." Wang notices with some disappointment that O-lan's feet are large because they had not been bound when she was young. The Old Mistress orders O-lan to obey her husband, bear him sons, and bring the first child for her to see. Then she abruptly dismisses them. This seems to be the entire marriage ceremony for a poor farmer and a slave bride.

The first things Wang does for O-lan are to carry her heavy box and buy her a few small, green peaches. To bring good fortune on his marriage and future, he lights two sticks of incense, one for O-lan and one for himself, before the earth god and goddess in the little field shrine. O-lan puts out her hand and brushes off the ashes so that the incense will burn well. To Wang it seems that O-lan is sharing a significant moment with him.

NOTE: Chinese society and tradition As the novel opens you come across a number of customs and traditions common in Chinese society before the People's Republic of China was established in 1949. The queue—or pigtail—worn by Chinese men was already being considered old-fashioned when the story of *The Good Earth* begins around 1890. But Wang Lung shows the importance of respecting his father (and other elders) when he says that he needs his father's permission to cut it off. Notice that Wang's wife was purchased and that she was a slave. You will see throughout the book that the birth of female children to poor families was considered a disaster. If parents didn't kill the infant— as O-lan does her fourth child—they would probably sell it at an early age as a slave, usually to the household of a rich man. A slave could become a wife, kitchen maid, or prostitute. In another traditional gesture, Wang burns incense to the little god and goddess of the earth to ask for good fortune.

At the farmhouse, O-lan cooks the wedding feast. The guests, all male, arrive, and O-lan declines to appear before them. But she has cooked a fine feast, and Wang is proud of both her modesty and her skill. Alone with her at last he is shy and nervous but finally exultant at having a sexual partner and a new life with a woman of his own.

NOTE: Some readers have observed that the first chapters of *The Good Earth* are beautifully written. Consider how skillfully Chapter 1 sets the scene and introduces all the major characters without once breaking the flow of the narrative. Notice that the chapter not only gives us the bare facts of Wang's way of life, but also the deeper feelings of some of the characters. A particularly touching moment occurs when Wang finds O-lan asleep in the straw beside the ox, like the kitchen slave she had been for ten of her twenty years. He must lead her by the hand into the room she will share with him as his wife.

CHAPTER 2

Wang Lung wakes to the brand new luxury of lying in bed while his wife lights the fire, heats the water, and brings him and his father steaming bowls of water. She has pleased him in their first night together, and he would like to know whether he pleases her. She puts no tea leaves in the old man's bowl but there is tea in Wang's. O-lan is afraid, for she has done this on her own. But Wang is pleased—it is a sign that she likes him.

O-lan takes over her household duties and the care of Wang's father. In addition, she gathers, without being asked, fuel from the roadside and manure at the crossroads and comes to hoe beside Wang in the field. In due course she becomes pregnant.

NOTE: In China it was the rule that when a woman married she left her family, or as in O-lan's case her owners, to reside in the household of her husband's family. If Wang's mother were alive, O-lan would be subservient to her as well as to her father-in-law and husband. One of the reasons that having a son was so crucial for a Chinese family was that it promised one would eventually have the service of a daughter-in-law.

By following O-lan through her duties you learn what the life of a peasant woman was like in traditional China, and you learn much about O-lan as well. The way she goes about her work and does what needs to be done without being told indicates that she is happy in her new life. She takes pride in her new household and wants it to run smoothly. Yet she doesn't talk. Wang Lung would like to know more of her past, but, according to Chinese custom, it would not be proper for a man to show much curiosity about his wife.

You see a strong bond growing between Wang

Lung and O-lan. Working beside her in the field, Wang falls into a rhythm of movement with her so that through the hours he doesn't feel the long, back-breaking labor. The paragraph describing the two of them working in harmony along the furrows of growing wheat is worth reading with care. It suggests the blend of pain and joy in their joint effort to make the earth productive and also the fatalism of their life close to the soil.

At the end of the chapter comes O-lan's announcement that she is pregnant. Wang is deeply moved—astonishingly, he has helped to create life.

CHAPTER 3

The time for O-lan to give birth draws near. Wang offers to have a woman come to help her from the village or perhaps from the Great House.

For the first time O-lan is angry, and words pour from her. She will return to that house only with her son in her arms, the baby in a red coat and flowered trousers and herself in new shoes and a coat of black satin. She has even counted out what money she will need, just three pieces of silver. Wang gives her four, so that she can make the baby's coat of silk—"After all, he is the first." O-lan, taking the money, says, "It is the first time I have silver money in my hand." Keep in mind this first appearance of silver, a valuable item that isn't land. You may want to consider it a bad omen in light of future events.

O-lan does not want a woman to help her. She works beside Wang in the field until her labor pains begin. He comes in from the field to find that she has put his hot supper on the table, but she endures the birth almost silently behind her closed door. When he hears a baby cry he begs through the door to know if it is a male, and she answers faintly that it is. Only then is he able to sit down and eat his now cold supper.

When at last she calls him in, all trace of the birth has been cleared away and the baby lies beside her, wrapped in a pair of its father's old trousers, as is the custom. Wang's heart is bursting for them both. Tomorrow he will buy red sugar to treat her to a celebratory drink. He will also fashion red-colored eggs to let all the neighbors know that he has a son.

NOTE: The color red   To the Chinese even today the color red is associated with happy events like New Year's Day, births, weddings, and anniversaries. Gifts of money are given in red envelopes, red garments are worn, and food or garnishes are red. This is probably the reason we associate the color with the Chinese. A particular shade is known as "Chinese red."

What strength it must have taken for O-lan to face the birth of her first child all alone! Why does she refuse Wang's offer to bring her a woman? Her anger at his mention of someone from the Great House tells you something—she was treated badly there, surely, and she must hate or mistrust the other women slaves. As for a village woman, does she recoil from that because she doesn't know any of them? You are not told. Apparently she has been present at a birth, because she knows she will need a reed, newly peeled and slit at its end "to cut the child's life from mine," that is, to cut the umbilical cord. She also knows that a boy is wrapped in his father's old trousers, a symbol of the child's own future as a father of sons.

The birth of Wang's first son is one of the book's deeply moving passages, with its stark image of a woman alone, dealing single-handedly with the fearful and exalting task of giving birth to a new life. You may well wonder how O-lan could be so sure that her baby would be a boy, when she dreamed of dressing him up to be presented at the Great House. At this point in the story you can't yet know the depth of disappointment if it had been a girl—a "slave" whose birth is an evil omen for a poor family since she cannot take over the land eventually but has to be fed until married and thereafter serves her husband's household.

Another fact of peasant life is revealed in this chapter, and it is a harsh fact indeed. Wang's father recalls the births that Wang's mother endured: a score or more, he forgets how many, and of them all only one—Wang—survived.

NOTE: At different times Pearl Buck worked closely with Chinese women. For a time she helped at an institution that took in slave girls who had fled cruel owners. Later she helped with her mother's work counseling Chinese women and listening to their problems. It's not surprising that the troubles of women in China find their way into what is mainly the story of a man.

CHAPTER 4

Wang buys the red sugar for O-lan's drink, the eggs to be colored, and—suddenly fearful of his fortune—four sticks of incense, one for each member of the family, to burn before the little earth gods.

Soon O-lan is working beside Wang again. The harvest is gathered, the threshing must be done, and then the fields need to be plowed and planted again for winter wheat. The baby sleeps on an old quilt on the ground, and when he wakes O-lan feeds him. Because she has an abundance of milk, the well-fed baby is fat and good-natured. The harvest, too, is plentiful. The little house is crowded with jars of woven reeds brimming with wheat and rice. Wang stores his surplus against winter and high prices. From the rafters hang strings of garlic and onions, and a leg of pork and two chickens that O-lan has salted down for the winter.

Wang Lung and O-lan celebrate their child's first month with a feast of noodles (for long life) and distribute the red-dyed eggs. The winter rains come, and the winter wheat sprouts. With no farm work to do, the farmers visit one another, drinking tea and gossiping. Wang Lung does little of this, however. Instead, he enjoys quiet hours spent mending farm implements, with O-lan nearby repairing earthen jars and household tools and making clothes and cloth shoes for the family. Husband and wife speak little but are content in each other's company.

When Wang Lung sells his produce he has a good handful of silver pieces above what they need. O-lan digs a hole in the earthen wall of their bedroom, Wang thrusts in the silver, and she closes the hole with a clod of earth.

Some disturbing comments are introduced into this scene of prosperity and contentment. Wang Lung doesn't want to let his neighbors see his plenty. They will be envious or ask to borrow. He is also afraid to let his neighbors know that he has silver hidden away. A contrast is drawn with his uncle, a lazy man and a gambler, and the uncle's equally lazy wife. Their house is ramshackle, their children are unruly, and the uncle sells his produce at the peak of harvest and at the lowest price for ready cash. You can expect to hear more of this shiftless uncle and his family. Remember to think about how silver is used to symbolize wealth apart from the land.

CHAPTER 5

The New Year, a time of celebration, is near. Wang Lung buys red paper brushed with the letters for happiness or riches and pastes them on his plow and his ox's yoke. He hangs strips of red paper with good luck mottoes on the doors and a paper flower over the doorway. His old father cuts out new robes of red paper for the little earth gods. O-lan makes fancy cakes to take to the Old Mistress on the second day of the New Year and plain cakes for the New Year's Day visits of Wang's uncle and the neighbors.

NOTE: Chinese New Year In China, as in other countries where Buddhism has been influential, the New Year is the most important holiday of the year. Houses are cleaned thoroughly and ritually rid of evil spirits, elaborate foods are prepared, and gifts are given. A sign of a man's wealth and status is how lavishly he entertains and the extent and value of the gifts he gives. In addition, there are firecrackers (to chase evil spirits) and dances, and rice cakes or steamed bread is eaten. In relation to the Western calendar, the Chinese New Year occurs between January 10 and February 19.

On the second day Wang Lung, O-lan, and their baby boy, dressed in the new clothes O-lan has made for them, go to the House of Hwang. This time the gateman treats Wang with respect and offers him tea while he escorts O-lan and the baby to the Old Mistress. O-lan returns looking contented.

However, she has seen signs that the House of Hwang is in trouble: the Old Mistress is wearing last year's coat. From the cook she has learned that the five sons—young lords—are spending money abroad "like waste water" and sending home their cast-off women to be cared for. In addition, the Old Lord has been adding one or two concubines a year to his string, while the Old Mistress consumes enough opium every day "to fill two shoes with silver." [In some editions this is gold.] Their third daughter is to be married, with a prince's ransom for a dowry and the most fashionable and expensive wardrobe. To cap this back-stairs gossip, the Old Mistress herself has told O-lan that they will sell some of their good rice land.

NOTE: *The Good Earth* contains many marvelous turns of phrase like those of the cook and the Old

Mistress. Pearl Buck's years in China yielded not
only a depth of understanding of the Chinese way
of life, but also rich figures of speech that must
surely be direct translations from the Chinese.

Wang impulsively declares that he will buy the
land. O-lan protests that it is too far away. Why
not buy the land which his uncle has to sell? His
uncle's land is no good, replies Wang. He has
farmed it for twenty years and put nothing back
into the land. No, he will buy Hwang's land. Then
O-lan agrees, saying, "Last year this time I was a
slave in that house."

Surprisingly it is O-lan, the silent one, who voices
the realization of how life has changed. Even Wang
Lung is not the same. He is no longer the timid
peasant who came to the House of Hwang a year
ago to claim his bride. Now he is a prosperous,
self-confident farmer with enough silver stowed
away to buy land belonging to the town's great
family, the best land in the neighborhood.

With this act, Wang Lung will embark on a new
course in life, stepping over a threshold that few
peasants in any country, let alone China, can ever
cross. From a poor subsistence farmer living on the
edge of survival, he is about to become a comfort-
able landowner. His wife's thrift and diligence,
added to his own, have made this possible. Without exchanging a word about it, he and O-lan are
both aware that they are working together at this
joint enterprise and that they are succeeding. Their
contentment with each other shines through their
quiet, almost wordless companionship.

You may see a further, more subtle change:

O-lan has now achieved equal status, at least privately, with her husband. She still observes the forms, still walks the proper six paces behind him. But now he discusses with her the great new project of buying land. She dares to offer an opposing opinion, and Wang Lung listens and answers her as he would answer an equal.

NOTE: A memorable scene in the film version of *The Good Earth* occurs in this chapter when Wang, walking home from Hwang's house, suddenly realizes that he is carrying his infant son and boasting of the baby's beauty where any passing evil spirit can strike at the child. He hastily hides the baby in his coat and talks of their worthless, pockmarked female child. Taking the cue, O-lan agrees.

Consider this reminder of evil spirits and the power of fortune to change things as you read the following chapters. As things change for Wang and O-lan, ask yourself whether it is really fortune (fate) or something else that destroys their happiness. Is it nature? Human nature? The times? Could Wang Lung have done anything (or not done anything) to avoid the next series of events?

CHAPTER 6

Wang Lung is depressed. His new land is more than a third of a mile from his farmhouse, a long walk to and from the day's work there. (It may not cheer him to remember that O-lan predicted this.) He misses the comfort of having silver hidden in the wall. And he bought the land, not from the

Old Lord, who was still sleeping although it was noon, but from the oily agent, thus missing all the glory of dealing with the head of the House of Hwang. It hurt him when the agent said that the silver that meant so much to Wang would buy a few days' opium for the Old Mistress. To Wang Lung the difference between him and the Great House seems as high as the city wall and as wide as the moat.

Spring comes with rain and wind, and Wang and O-lan toil in the fields from dawn to dark. She is pregnant again and Wang is cross with her. The birth will come at harvest when he will need her help. She says this birth will be nothing—only the first is hard.

As she predicts, she gives birth in the morning and is back beside him by afternoon, gathering the sheaves. He would like to send her home to rest, but his weariness makes him unkind and he only asks about the child's sex. It is a boy.

Again the harvest is good. All the village now knows that Wang Lung is prospering.

Wang Lung is not always a gentle, considerate husband. When he is overworked he can be rough. On this day he has not even stopped at midday to rest and eat because a thunderstorm threatens and the harvest must be cut and bound before the storm. He sees that O-lan is tired when she comes back to the field after giving birth. But he thinks he has suffered as much this day with his toil as she has with her childbirth.

Do you think O-lan carries her courage and independence too far? Would she get more kindness from Wang Lung if she showed a little weakness? You might think that she could just as well have stayed in the house and rested, instead of venturing out again to help him.

Would you say that Pearl Buck is telling you something further about O-lan? Might she want you to see that O-lan cares as much as Wang about their land, their harvest, and their prosperity, that she is willing, as he is, to work to exhaustion in their joint effort to rise from poverty?

In the next chapter Buck offers a contrast between O-lan and a different kind of farmer's wife, the wife of Wang's uncle.

CHAPTER 7

Wang Lung is disgusted with the way his uncle's children run wild in the village street. He meets the eldest, a girl of fifteen, her hair uncombed, talking immodestly with men. Wang goes to the girl's mother and protests.

The uncle's wife is too lazy to sweep her floor but she has a lively tongue. It's all very well, she says, for those who have too much land and money to buy still more. But her husband has an evil destiny. For him nothing grows but weeds. Then the uncle himself comes to Wang to complain of his bad luck. He scolds Wang for criticizing him and threatens to spread it through the village that Wang has been disrespectful. In the end Wang gives him money, supposedly for a matchmaker to find a husband for the uncle's eldest girl, but as Wang knows, really for his uncle to gamble away.

Meanwhile O-lan has given birth again, to a daughter this time. Back in his field, Wang sees a flight of crows, an evil omen.

The scenes with the uncle and the uncle's wife

could be comedy but it would be dark comedy.
You may know people like them, who blame bad
luck for all their troubles. You are forewarned that
in time this uncle and his family will create even
bigger problems for Wang. Meanwhile the omens
multiply. A girl is born: "Only a slave this time—
not worth mentioning," says O-lan. When Wang
tells her he has lent money to his uncle, she says,
"It is better not to say lend," because she knows
it will never be repaid.

NOTE: Consider the matter of the evil omens.
Do you think Wang may have seen flights of crows
on other occasions and never noticed them? This
time, however, he has already had the encounter
with his uncle, which cost him money, and the
birth of a daughter, which in Chinese eyes is a
misfortune, so perhaps he is ready to see evil omens
everywhere.

CHAPTER 8

Wang reaps a good harvest of rice, and with the
silver from its sale he buys another piece of land
from the nearly destitute House of Hwang. But
with the spring comes one of the region's periodic
droughts. Wang's pond dries up, his crops fail,
and even the rice lands that he cares for labori-
ously do not yield a crop.

Meanwhile O-lan becomes pregnant again so that
her milk dries and she is unable to feed her baby
girl. With the food stores gone, the ox must be
killed to feed the family. Wang can't bring himself

to slaughter the animal that has shared his work for so long, so O-lan performs the dread task. Were you surprised at O-lan's strength? What do you already know about Wang and O-lan's characters that prepared you for this incident?

As expected, Wang's uncle comes begging for food. The first time, Wang gives him a handful of beans and corn. The second time, he does not dare to share what little is left to feed his own family. The uncle spreads word in the village that his nephew has food and refuses to share. Stirred up, the neighbors raid Wang's house and take his last small store of beans and corn. They are about to take his furniture when O-lan intervenes. "You still have your furniture," she says, "Leave us ours."

Now Wang Lung comforts himself. If he still had the silver or had bought food with it, the neighbors would have taken it all. Instead he bought land, and they couldn't take that from him. Here again the value of land is superior to mere money. The author seems to excuse Wang's neighbors for raiding his house and stealing his little store of food. Of them she writes, "They are not bad people, except when they are starving." Can you see a justification for the breakdown of law and morality in a time of disaster?

NOTE: You have frequently read in the newspapers and seen on television accounts of drought and starvation in Africa and India. Today prosperous nations contribute to the relief of the starving. When *The Good Earth* takes place, however, the outside world hardly heard of the periodic famines in China. In that vast country a drought might strike one region while others had plentiful rain and good harvests. Once during Pearl Buck's childhood, starving refugees from the north poured into Chinkiang, the site of her parents' mission. Buck's mother protested angrily that there was plenty of food in other parts of China and asked why they couldn't feed their own hungry people. The lack of a strong central government and provincial selfishness provided at least part of the answer.

CHAPTER 9

All the animals in the village have been eaten, even the stray dogs. Wang's neighbor Ching says that in the village people are eating human flesh. Wang decides that his family will migrate south. O-lan says to wait only a day and she will have given birth. Ching brings a handful of dried beans to help O-lan through her childbirth. Wang saves a few beans to feed his starving baby daughter.

O-lan gives birth, alone as before, and the newborn, a girl, is dead. Wang sees from bruises on the infant that O-lan has strangled the baby because she can't feed it. Wang takes the body out to bury, but he is too weak to dig a grave in the dry, hardened earth.

NOTE: Were you shocked by O-lan's action in killing her baby? Would you have counseled her otherwise? Pearl Buck saw the effects of famine during her childhood in China. She must also have known of the practice of female infanticide among

poor women. A baby girl was considered worthless, only another mouth to feed or at best a slave
you could sell later on.

Infanticide, the killing of newborn babies, has
been known in many parts of the world in both
ancient and modern times. In some cultures it was
an accepted custom and not against the law. The
Romans, as well as the Spartans of ancient Greece,
put unwanted infants in the wilderness to die of
exposure or be killed by wild animals.

Wang's uncle brings two strange men who offer
to buy Wang's land for a fraction of its worth. Wang
sees his second son crawling, too weak to stand,
and is tempted, but then bursts into tears of weakness and anger and refuses. O-lan backs him up.
They will not sell the land, but they will sell the
furniture. She accepts the two pieces of silver the
men pay her, scarcely the price of one bed. Now,
she says, it is time to go.

Wang's uncle appears well fed. His three youngest children have disappeared; he does not say
where. The implication is that the uncle and his
wife, like others in the village, have taken to cannibalism. The uncle shows no shame, except that
he remains out of sight while the two speculators
put his own elder brother, Wang's father, on the
floor and take the old man's bed.

CHAPTER 10

Wang and his family leave their stripped house.
They are skin and bones, and the children's bellies
are swollen from malnutrition. They take only the

clothes they wear, except that O-lan gives each of her small sons a bowl and chopsticks, a promise of food to come. Wang carries his frail little girl until he sees his father stumbling and about to fall. He then gives the child to O-lan and takes his father on his back. They pass the Great House, its gates shut tight and a few famished people huddled there.

Outside the town, Wang and his family join the flood of refugees. They are heading for the "fire-wagon," the railroad train. When the train comes the crowd pushes them along, clinging together, into the railroad car.

CHAPTER 11

The desperate journey continues. Wang pays the fare for the hundred mile trip south with his two pieces of silver, and buys a little food with some of the change. A man in the train, who has been through this before, advises Wang to save a few coppers for mats to build a shelter. There are public kitchens where the poor can buy cooked rice, as much as one can eat for a penny. They must get the rest of their food by begging. Wang will not beg. Well, then he can wear himself out taxiing the rich in a two-wheeled, hand-pulled riksha.

They reach the city, and all turns out as the man on the train said. O-lan, ever resourceful, remembers from her childhood how to make a hut against a wall where others have built theirs. They eat their rice at the soup kitchen, then go back to their shelter and fall into exhausted sleep.

The next morning Wang looks to O-lan to say what should be done. Again, she remembers. She leads the little boys and the old man out to the street where they will hold out their bowls and call to passersby. When the little boys consider it a game, she spanks them soundly until, with tear-streaked faces, they are fit to beg.

Wang Lung rents a riksha and learns that he must bargain with a customer for a fare. At the day's end he has only one penny left above the riksha rental. The old man sits by the roadside, dozing and forgetting to beg. But O-lan and the little boys have begged enough to buy the family's rice in the morning. Do you think Wang's refusal to beg is realistic?

After the horror of the starving village, the change of scene is welcome. With Wang and his family you have your first glimpse of a teeming city. Here food is plentiful and people of means provide something for the poor. The policeman at the food kitchen answers Wang's questions: the rich do this to win people's good opinion or acquire merit in heaven. But some must do it out of a good heart? To this Wang gets no answer.

Wang's old father is both amusing and touching, good-humored, determined to survive, certain that his son and grandsons will care for him. But what do you think of O-lan's impressive performance under stress? She has now taken charge of the family's welfare, and even Wang Lung looks to her for guidance. You might consider whether the family would have survived to this point without her firmness of will and her calm, practical approach to each situation, however strange or shocking. Note also how the second son's character is forecast, as he refuses to give up the money he got by begging. He sleeps with it clutched in his hand and pays for his rice himself the next day.

This first day in the city reveals the ironic fate of the working poor. Wang Lung's hands are blistered as he drops with exhaustion, yet O-lan has taken in more money by begging than he has with his grueling toil.

CHAPTER 12

Wang Lung is getting to know the city, taking passengers to schools, markets, and houses of business and pleasure. He smells tempting cooking odors, hears music and the click of dice but never sees what is going on inside buildings. When a street orator calls for revolution against foreigners, Wang is frightened, thinking he and his family are those foreigners.

NOTE: The Boxer Uprising The reference to the oration against foreigners is probably a reference to the movement known as the Boxer Uprising (or Boxer Rebellion), which called for the removal of foreigners from China. Foreign traders had gradually acquired certain rights to do business in China and during the early nineteenth century had forced the Chinese imperial government to grant them more and more concessions by threat of force. The Boxers, as they were called in English, gained popularity and strength by intriguing with the Empress Dowager against the Emperor and in 1899–1900 outbreaks of violence against Europeans occurred. Pearl Buck herself experienced this threat as a little girl. The rebellion was eventually crushed by the intervention of the Western powers and Japan.

One day Wang Lung has a strange-looking passenger—is this male or female?—who turns out to be an American woman. She pays him double the fare and rebukes him for running himself to death. He is amazed at the abundance and variety of food in the markets. Surely no one could starve in this city! Yet every dawn, he and his family join a long line of people for their penny bowl of thin rice gruel at the public kitchens.

In this and the other chapters that describe Wang's sojourn in the city, Pearl Buck analyzes the nature of urban wealth, how it is based on wage labor that dooms the workers to hopeless poverty. Do you think the desperate condition of farmers is different from this? The author also is commenting on the nature of public welfare. Is it suggested that welfare is a permanent condition in cities or only a stopgap in times of crisis? Is there anything else about the description of city life that supports Wang's preference for the land? What about the moral tone?

Even with Wang Lung's work and O-lan's begging, they have enough to cook a little supper in their hut only when the boys have snatched a bit of fuel from a farm wagon. Wang is worried that his second son is becoming adept at stealing. He tells himself that they must get back to the land. But how?

NOTE: Amid the hardship, Pearl Buck has a little fun in this chapter with the American woman in Wang's riksha. Did Buck sketch herself into this scene, as the film director Alfred Hitchcock always put himself into one of his own scenes? Buck was a tall woman and she may well have worn a long black coat, but she certainly did not speak broken Chinese. Still, one can imagine her telling the riksha puller that he needn't run himself to death. How would you feel, sitting in a carriage pulled by a man so thin he was obviously half-starved? You wouldn't like being pulled by a pitifully thin horse, let alone a man.

CHAPTER 13

Running about the city all day, Wang Lung becomes more and more aware of the gap between the rich and the poor who serve them. In the slum around their hut, children are born and die with such frequency that even their parents scarcely know how many there have been. O-lan is pregnant again. With spring in the air, Wang longs for the fields which he should be plowing. If they had something to sell, he tells O-lan, they could go home now. O-lan answers that they have something, their daughter. The little girl has grown and filled out, and is learning to walk although she doesn't talk.

A neighbor who works all night pulling heavy supply wagons into the city tells them he has sold two daughters and will sell a third if the child his wife is now carrying turns out to be a girl. Others kill their newborn daughters but he sells his. He has sold one to the mansion on the other side of the wall, a rich man's house where even the servants eat with ivory and silver chopsticks.

Wang Lung considers selling his small daughter. She would be fed and clothed, and he would be able to take the family back to the land. This is one of the ways to survive, when the poor are too poor. But his neighbor also says ominously, "When the rich are too rich, there are ways."

Pearl Buck here draws her sharpest picture of the desperation of the city's poor. Wang's old father has been through times like this twice in his youth but each time he returned to the land because it is always there. Wang has almost decided to sell his small daughter. He doesn't wonder about his neighbor's second piece of wisdom, about what happens when the rich are too rich. But to you this is a promise. After wondering how Wang and his family can ever escape from this situation, you might now expect some dramatic turn in their story.

CHAPTER 14

Leaflets are handed out by speakers on the street. One leaflet shows Jesus, another depicts a fat rich man standing over a worker who is skin and bones. Christianity and Communism were two of the alternatives being offered the desperate. Both, you should notice, were systems foreign to China. Wang understands nothing of all this. But one day he sees soldiers dragging away men like himself. The shopkeeper who hides him explains that the soldiers are capturing the men in preparation for a battle nearby. Wang Lung, to avoid being seized, changes his work to hauling the heavy wagons at night, for half as much as he made with his riksha. Meanwhile O-lan and the boys see people in silks and wagonloads of their possessions leaving the city. Presently the market stalls are bare and the shops shut.

With his daughter in his lap, thinking that he must sell her, Wang Lung asks O-lan about her life as a slave. She tells him she was beaten every day. And the pretty slaves? They were taken to the young lords' beds and then given to the men servants, while they were still children. Wang Lung, horrified, can still think of no other way to return to his land but to sell the girl. Suddenly his burly neighbor calls out that the rich man's gates are open. O-lan quickly steals away. Wang is swept through the gates with the mob.

While the mob fights over the richly painted boxes of clothing, bedding, dishes, and household goods, Wang comes upon a fat man, richly dressed, who was too slow to escape. The man begs for his life, offering money in return. Wang takes all the man's money and lets him go, then hurries back to the hut, rejoicing: "Tomorrow we go back to the land!"

Here Pearl Buck gives us another stunning picture, this time of the fleeing rich, the shut-down city, and the famished poor falling upon the possessions of the rich. She even gives us a moment of comedy when Wang Lung, who was too softhearted to kill an ox to feed his starving children, thunders at the fat man after taking all his money, "Out of my sight, lest I kill you for a fat worm!" Now Wang Lung has what he could never have achieved by his back-breaking toil and O-lan's begging: an escape from poverty. Pearl Buck seems to indicate that only by plundering the rich can the poor escape their hopeless condition. What do you think now of the morals of Wang Lung, who punished his second son for stealing a bit of meat but feels no guilt in extorting the rich man's money? Or will Wang pay a high price in the future for this act? What grows out of this seed money when he returns to his village?

CHAPTER 15

Wang Lung and his family are on their way home. He has bought good seed for some luxury crops as well as the basics. In his joy he pays too much for an ox that takes his fancy. At the house, his farm tools, the door, and the thatch are all gone. His neighbor Ching tells him that a robber band, with whom Wang's uncle had some connection, had lived in the house. The uncle sold his daughter and left with his wife and son, no one knows where. Ching's wife died of starvation and he gave his daughter to a soldier to keep her alive. Ching himself, thin as a shadow and barely alive, has nothing left. Wang gives his friend seed and will bring his ox to help plow and plant Ching's field.

With O-lan, Wang goes into the town to buy furniture and farm tools. He also buys a new paper god of wealth to hang on the wall, along with candlesticks, an incense urn, and thick red candles to burn before it. He seems to forget his loyalty to the land and he speaks angrily to the little earth gods in the field. Later, however, fearful for his new happiness, he decides to win them over and burns some incense to them.

In this happy scene, you find in rich detail how Wang Lung restores his house and land, how he repays Ching who shared with him his last few beans, and how he sets up a shrine to give thanks to the god of wealth. His familiar relationships with the small field gods add the kind of comedy that Pearl Buck manages to draw out of her situations

without seeming to make fun of her characters.
You may well find enough such comedy to make
a study of the humor in this realistic, often harsh
and painful story.

CHAPTER 16

It is now revealed that O-lan has a bag of jewels
hidden in her bosom, stolen from the rich man's
house in the city. She asks to keep only two small
pearls, and Wang takes the rest. He goes at once
to the House of Hwang. He will put the treasure
into the one thing robbers can't take—more land.

The Old Lord himself comes to the gate,
shrunken, coughing, his fur-trimmed satin gown
dirty and bedraggled. He alone is left, with the
slave woman Cuckoo to look after him. Cuckoo
tells Wang that all the servants have fled during
the famine but some came back as robbers to plunder the mansion. The Old Mistress died of the fright
they gave her. The young lords want to sell all 300
acres that are left.

Wang Lung goes to the town to drink tea with
the shopkeeper and hear the news. The man con-
firms what Cuckoo has told him. Wang Lung goes
back to buy the land.

This picture of the fall of a once great family is
dramatic. Like nature, might not families be ruled
by cycles of poverty and prosperity? The author is
preparing you for the story of Wang Lung's own
rise and fall. How is a family's fate connected to
nature in this book? Remember that the Hwang
fortunes had begun to fail even before the Old
Lord's time because no one cared about the land.

At this point Wang remembers how even the
thought of the Old Lord intimidated him in the

past. Now the old man is not even as impressive as Wang's own father, who at least is a clean and smiling old man.

O-lan's resourcefulness, in knowing where to look for jewels in a rich man's house and how to keep them hidden, has now made Wang Lung's fortune. Once more O-lan's importance to the family is underscored.

CHAPTER 17

Wang Lung's lands are now too broad for him to farm alone. He buys Ching's small property and takes Ching to live with his family and work with him. At harvest time he hires farm laborers and makes Ching his overseer. Wang builds a second house behind the first, leaving the old farmhouse to Ching and the farm workers. He sets himself the goal of laying up enough stores in the good years to survive any future years of drought and flood.

Although he no longer allows O-lan to work in the field, he takes his two sons out with him, hoping to inspire them with his own love of the land. When Wang fails in this, and when his own illiteracy becomes embarrassing because he must sign contracts he can't read, he enrolls the two boys in a school in the town. The old teacher gives the boys school names suitable to their father's calling—Nung En and Nung Wen. "Nung" means that the family's wealth is from the earth. Is this wealth from the earth as you see it? How was Wang able to buy all this land?

NOTE: You can make an interesting list of what constitutes prosperity to a typical Chinese farmer like Wang Lung: a new house with a tiled roof instead of a thatched one and whitewash on the earthen walls, a separate storeroom for his crops, farm laborers and an overseer, pigs and fowl in the farmyard to provide meat for his table, and not the least, two sons in school.

O-lan has given birth to twins—"an egg with a double yolk," Wang's old father jokes. Wang now has five children, three boys and two girls. His elder daughter hasn't learned to talk or do the things appropriate to her age, and he knows now that she suffered permanent damage in her development during the famine. He calls her his "poor little fool" and remembers how close he came to selling her. If he had, he realizes now, her owners would have killed her as useless.

NOTE: Pearl Buck's sympathetic portrait of the relationship between Wang and his retarded daughter stems in no small part from the fact that her daughter Carol was retarded. The author devoted much effort to helping the mentally retarded. In the book, Wang is the only one who cares about the little girl. Given what you already know about traditional Chinese attitudes toward female children as drains on the family's food supply, is it likely in reality that Wang would have such fondness for her? Is this just the author's feelings coming through or is Wang's personality consistent with this devotion?

Wang himself rarely works on the land now, having others to do the work and being busy with the commerce of selling his crops. O-lan has had a hard birth this time, with twins. Is it possible that she has pushed her self-reliance too far, that having no help with the birth was unwise? Would you agree with those who say her insistence on doing it all by herself was not strength but stubbornness? What do you make of this aspect of O-lan's character?

CHAPTER 18

It is the seventh year of Wang Lung's prosperity, and disaster has again come to the region. This time it is a flood, with two-fifths of the land lying under water through the spring and summer. Many houses have been washed away and hunger is widespread, but Wang Lung's houses are safe on their hill and his storerooms are still full. He puts his hired laborers to work mending roofs, repairing implements, doing tasks he would be doing when field work was not possible. Now he finds himself idle and restless.

In the following chapters, you will begin to see how this idleness leads Wang even farther away from his origins and from his early happiness as a farmer, husband, and father.

NOTE: Pearl Buck may be recalling a part of her upbringing in a missionaries' household when she gives Wang seven years of prosperity. In the Old Testament, Joseph—Pharaoh's slave—interprets his master's dream as a prophecy of seven prosperous years followed by seven "lean" ones.

For the first time since he brought her home as a bride, Wang Lung looks at O-lan as a woman and sees that she has not cared for her appearance. When he rebukes her for this, she confesses that she has not been well since the birth of the twins. She sees him looking at her feet and she hides them under the bench, saying that she will bind their younger daughter's feet. The more humbly she answers him, the more ashamed he is at reproaching her and the angrier he becomes that she does not answer him with anger. How do you think she should have answered him? Is there anything she can say or do to change the way he feels toward her now?

Disgusted with her and himself, Wang rushes out to the tea shop. But the old tea shop now seems dingy, and he goes to a new tea shop, which is also a gambling den and brothel. Here he finds Cuckoo, formerly Hwang's slave, who is now hostess. She taunts him for drinking tea when he could drink wine, play at dice, enjoy the pretty women upstairs. She shows him the women's pictures on scrolls hanging on the tea shop walls. They are not dream women, as he thought, but real, and he may choose any one he likes. A slender one with a pretty face and a lotus bud in her hand attracts him, and he leaves excited but without pursuing his desire.

NOTE: Some readers find it hard to believe that Wang Lung can be so ignorant about prostitution, especially after his experience as a riksha puller in the city. Do you agree with them? Or do you think that what he displays is not ignorance but inexperience in this unfamiliar world of sexual pleasure for sale?

CHAPTER 19

With nothing new at home to distract him, Wang Lung goes again to the tea shop, and this time Cuckoo takes him upstairs to Lotus Flower. Cuckoo calls her "the little pink-faced dwarf from Soochow," but to Wang she is pure enchantment. She introduces him to sophisticated lovemaking.

Wang Lung now spends his days waiting for his nights with Lotus. No matter how much time he spends with her, he remains unsatisfied. O-lan and his children are silent around him, and his old father asks him what sickness he has that makes him bad-tempered and turns his skin so yellow (pale).

Wang begins bathing every day with scented soap. He has the barber cut off the long old-fashioned braid that you saw in Chapter 1 and he uses perfumed oil on his hair. He gives up the farmhouse smell of garlic. He has the town tailor make him fine clothes, and he buys his first store-bought shoes. He reminds O-lan of the sons of Hwang in the Great House. He is flattered. The comparison with the Hwang family is yet another reminder of what may be in store for him.

He is spending money wildly, for his hours with Lotus and for expensive gifts that she coaxes out of him. Finally he demands O-lan's two small pearls, the only things of value she has asked to keep.

Although she has cherished them, she gives them up without a word. When Wang has gone, her tears fall unchecked on his clothes that she is washing. Wang Lung is close to ruining himself in his infatuation with Lotus. O-lan does not protest although he is spending the silver stored in its hiding place. She is afraid of the anger that he turns on her constantly. His demand for the pearls leaves her heartbroken, yet she submits. This break with O-lan is the second of Wang's breaks with his past—the first was when he stopped working the land. In the next chapter another blow to his family life will arrive in the form of his uncle's evil family.

CHAPTER 20

Suddenly Wang's uncle reappears and brings his wife and son to live in Wang's house. As a nephew, Wang can't refuse to take them in, but he burns with rage.

The wife of Wang Lung's uncle reads the signs that O-lan failed to understand. One woman who has worn herself out for him is not enough for a man, and if he has money he will buy himself a second woman. The uncle's wife will help Wang buy Lotus from the House of Flowers.

NOTE: A concubine in Chinese society was a recognized second wife whose principal function was to serve her master sexually. Concubinage was an ancient custom in China, dating from the time of Confucius (about the sixth century B.C.) and it existed in various forms in other societies. A concubine might be a slave already in the man's household or one that he bought from a tea house, as Wang Lung bought Lotus Flower. A concubine lived in her own quarters and had no household duties. To have a concubine was evidence of wealth and brought a man respect and status in the community.

Wang has a cluster of new rooms added to his house, around a courtyard with a goldfish pond. But he is impatient. He scolds O-lan for not brushing her hair. To his astonishment she bursts into tears, something she has never done before in his presence. "I have borne you sons," she speaks out. Isn't this a Chinese wife's ultimate vindication? Notice that she makes no reference to his cruel behavior. He is again ashamed of his desire for Lotus.

At last the wife of Wang's uncle has made the deal: silver for the tea-house master, jewels and silks for Lotus, something for herself. Lotus arrives in a sedan chair and totters on her useless bound feet into her apartment. Cuckoo comes along as her servant.

O-lan deals with this situation by staying away with her children the entire day. At evening she returns, prepares the meal, eats with the children, then washes and goes to bed alone in the room she has shared with Wang Lung these many years. Wang goes to Lotus.

CHAPTER 21

Wang Lung has heard of the trouble with a first wife because of a second one, but O-lan simply ignores the existence of Lotus, whom she never sees, as Lotus keeps to her own quarters. Trouble arises between O-lan and Cuckoo, who was bossy and arrogant toward O-lan when she was a mere kitchen slave and Cuckoo was the Old Lord's servant. O-lan wants to know why she must have this woman in her house. When she gets no satisfaction from Wang (who doesn't know how to answer her) she takes it out on Cuckoo, who must share the kitchen with her. Wang solves the dispute by building a separate kitchen in Lotus' court.

Other annoyances arise. The uncle's wife begins visiting Lotus, entertaining her with gossip and sharing her more elegant food. Wang's father, catching sight of the painted silk-clad Lotus, roars that there is a harlot in the house. The last straw comes when Wang hears Lotus screaming at his retarded daughter whom the twins have innocently taken to see the mysterious lady. Lotus now shows the bad temper of which she is capable, calling his children filthy and cursing them. Wang will not tolerate this. He stays away from Lotus for two days. When he returns she does everything to please him, but it seems clear that his infatuation is waning.

Meanwhile the floods have receded. Wang throws off his city clothes and calls to Ching to bring the hoe, the plow, and the seeds—it's time to plant the winter wheat!

NOTE: Wang learns that a rich man's life is not peaceful—it bristles with annoyances. You probably will find some of these scenes comic, although no one who participates in them is amused. O-lan succeeds in getting Cuckoo out of her sight. Wang's old father, usually so good-natured, takes a cunning pleasure in shouting through Lotus' doorway or spitting on the tiles of her court. Wang will not have Lotus, a mere second wife, scream at his children, whom he loves, and especially not at his "poor fool." His call to Ching to come out and plant the winter wheat is a signal that he is freeing himself from his bondage to Lotus. As you can see, the return to the good earth is the medicine which always restores Wang Lung.

CHAPTER 22

Wang Lung comes in from his day in the fields, weary but triumphant, his spirits lifted. He goes to Lotus with earth still clinging to his hands and clothing, teases her about being a farmer's wife, and leaves laughing at her. He eats heartily, and laughs at Lotus again when she protests at his garlicky breath.

In the village he is now a man of importance. His uncle boasts of Wang's house and his wealth. The villagers borrow money from Wang and ask his advice in marrying off their children and settling disputes. His eldest son reads contracts for him and even corrects errors in them, while Wang stands by proudly.

But this boy is staying out of school and he weeps when rebuked. O-lan suggests he have a slave woman. Wang will not buy his son a slave but decides it is time to find him a wife.

Here you see Wang Lung at his best, a mature man in his prime, in control of his household affairs and with the wisdom and authority to advise others. He has restored his balance and refreshed his spirit by renewing his deep bond with the land. He has put Lotus in her place as a concubine, and restored O-lan to her proper place. She is his respected first wife, the mother of his children, the woman who keeps his household in order and looks after his and the family's well-being.

These two women are as sharply contrasted in character as in the roles that society has assigned them. O-lan is serious, responsible, undemanding. She rarely smiles and speaks only when she has something important to say. Lotus is lazy, self-indulgent, peevish when her wishes are not quickly granted, and given to sharp temper when she is crossed. Although both women were sold as slaves in childhood, one becomes a true wife, the other a courtesan. What do you think accounts for the different futures of these two girls?

You may find further points for comparison in Wang's two daughters, one nearly sold as a slave and the other now being groomed for marriage. They are both of the same family, but the family's fortunes have abruptly changed from poverty to prosperity, and so there is never a question of the second daughter being sold as a slave.

Meanwhile, O-lan's solution for her son's unhappiness is to buy a slave for him, that is, to give him a sexual outlet. Do you find this surprising in light of her own slavery and her contempt for Cuckoo, who performed this function for the Old Lord? Or is it just one more example of O-lan's practical solutions for problems?

CHAPTER 23

From Lotus, surprisingly, Wang Lung learns of a suitable bride for his eldest son, the daughter of the respectable grain merchant Liu, who was a client of the House of Flowers tea house. Cuckoo offers to make the match. Meanwhile, the boy comes home drunk after a night with a prostitute, and Wang Lung orders his uncle, the wife, and their son—who is corrupting his own son—out of his house. But his uncle slyly shows Wang the false beard he wears as a member of a gang of local bandits, the notorious Redbeards. Wang is trapped. He must keep this uncle and his family in the house as protection against the gang.

A natural echo of this unnatural human evil arrives in the form of a plague of locusts, which again drives Wang back to the land. He organizes his workers and the younger farmers to fight the swarms of locusts. They battle for seven days and nights, saving some of the harvest. Although the villagers and O-lan serve the locusts roasted or fried, Wang will not eat these enemies of the land. By showing that such natural enemies have some good use, isn't the author making another strong contrast between natural calamities and the evil behavior that causes only misery? The fight to save his fields and the return to the land has brought Wang calm.

CHAPTER 24

Wang's eldest son wants to leave the land and go south to the university. Wang is angry and compares his tall, slim son with fine skin and soft hands to himself, thick-bodied and sunburnt. He roars at his son to work in the fields so as not to be mistaken for a woman. But O-lan tells Wang indirectly that this son is spending time with Lotus, and she advises that the youth be sent south as he asks. Wang catches his son and Lotus talking together. In a towering rage he beats them both. Lotus pleads with him, assuring him that the boy comes only to talk to her. Wang Lung calms down and gives the boy permission to leave home.

What do you think of Wang Lung's behavior toward his son? As a youth Wang Lung had to work in the fields or starve. But as the son of a well-to-do farmer, this youth has nothing to do. In the isolated countryside he apparently has no friends and nowhere to go for entertainment, except the forbidden places the uncle's son has led him to. Wang's own youth was so different that he seems to have little understanding of his son's emotional needs.

In this chapter a contrast is again drawn between O-lan and Lotus, this time in terms of what the passing years have done to each. Living a soft life, Lotus has become rounded, less fragile and more beautiful. O-lan is now gaunt and worn, and her abdomen is swollen, apparently with a tumor. Wang Lung still takes her for granted and doesn't notice that she is dragging herself painfully about her duties.

CHAPTER 25

Wang Lung now considers the situation of his second son. This boy has also scorned working in the fields and demands to be sent to school like his brother. Otherwise he is very unlike the eldest son. Slightly built, crafty, and with a touch of malicious humor, he reminds Wang of his own father. This boy should make a good merchant. Wang apprentices him to the grain merchant Liu, to whose daughter the eldest son is already betrothed. At the same time Wang arranges a betrothal between his second daughter, now ten, and a son of Liu's who is the same age.

This daughter is a pretty child who walks gracefully on her bound feet, but cries from the pain she has to endure. Although Wang is kind and would let her have her feet unbound, the girl knows she must go on or "My husband would not love me even as you do not love my mother."

NOTE: On foot-binding Foot-binding, a peculiarly Chinese custom, arose in early China as a way for women to please men with their tiny feet and to enhance the man's status by this evidence that his wife or concubine didn't need to work. You might compare bound feet with the "wasp" waists that were fashionable for Western women in the last century. A man could circle his two hands around such a narrow waist, which a woman achieved only by wearing tight corsets that squeezed and displaced her internal organs. Understandably, many women suffered injury and illness. Foot-binding, although more crippling, had the same purpose—to please men.

The origin of foot-binding has been traced to the T'ang Dynasty (A.D. 618 to 907), a time of high artistic achievement in the imperial court. According to legend, a favorite court dancer bound her

feet to squeeze them into small dancing shoes. The
style caught on among the well-to-do. The practice
began when a little girl was five or six. Her feet
were bound in cloth to force the toes and heel to
curl under, causing the arch and instep to rise un-
naturally. Periodically the bindings were tight-
ened.

Wang is stung by the truth of his daughter's
remark and remorseful at his treatment of O-lan.
Furthermore, he now realizes that O-lan is ill. He
sends her to lie down and goes for the doctor.

The doctor, who prescribes a broth of herbs, will
charge 500 pieces of silver for a cure. O-lan says
that her life is not worth that much, a sum that
could buy a good piece of land. Wang protests that
he has the money. But the doctor, knowing that
the illness is fatal, says he must charge not 500 but
5000 pieces of silver for a cure. Wang understands.
The silver that can buy more land cannot buy life;
nature, unlike men, cannot be changed by riches
the way riches can change men.

CHAPTER 26

O-lan's illness lasts through the winter. Wang
Lung stays away from Lotus and sits continually
at O-lan's bedside, watching over her even though
he feels no real tenderness for her.

Meanwhile, the household falls into disorder.
Wang Lung realizes how much work O-lan did
without complaint, how much comfort she brought
to them all, how competent and caring she was.
Again it is O-lan, in a conscious interlude, who
solves the family's problem: she asks that her fu-

ture daughter-in-law be brought to the house to take charge.

O-lan has Cuckoo summoned and she speaks her mind to this woman who once lorded over her. O-lan asks to see her son married before she dies, and Wang Lung sends for him. He is now fully grown, tall and well built, and Wang Lung is proud of him. He is cheerful with his mother although his eyes fill with tears.

Cuckoo, Lotus, and the uncle's wife prepare the bride for her wedding, and Wang Lung gives a large feast. At O-lan's request, the pair eat their rice and drink their wine at her bedside, and she has her door kept open so that she can hear the sounds of the wedding feast. She instructs the bridal couple in their duties to their father, their grandfather, the poor retarded daughter, "and no other," a pointed reference to Lotus. Later, half conscious, she reminds Wang Lung of a wife's true role when she murmurs, "And if I am ugly, still I have borne a son," and again she reproaches him with a reminder that "beauty will not bear a man sons!" With Wang Lung beside her she dies.

NOTE: Murmuring on her deathbed, O-lan tells us more of her life than she ever did when she was well. You can figure out her age: she was twenty when she became Wang's wife and her son, born during her first year of marriage, was eighteen when he left home and may be nineteen or twenty when he returns. Considering her hard life as a child slave and then a farm wife, it is perhaps not surprising that she should be no more than forty years old when she dies.

To emphasize the change in Wang Lung's life, his aged father dies soon after. Walking home from the joint burial, he wishes he had not taken those two pearls from O-lan to give to Lotus. He thinks that with O-lan's burial he has buried half his life. Alone where no one sees him, he weeps. Wang Lung has unhappy feelings about the room he shared with O-lan through the good years of their marriage, so he gives that room to the newlyweds and moves to Lotus' quarters.

Thus, without two of the central figures of his old family, he begins the second half of his life.

NOTE: You are present at two ritual events in this chapter, a wedding and a funeral, and you witness both in detail. One such detail, and part of the traditional religious lore, is Wang's consultation with a local wise man, called a geomancer, to determine a lucky day for the burials. How important is ritual in the novel? What do you think its function is in Chinese society?

CHAPTER 27

The land is again flooded in another natural catastrophe. Wang's houses on the hill stand above as if on an island and the village can be reached only by boat. Farmers once again take their families south as refugees from the famine. Wang has enough food, so the uncle's wife and son goad the uncle into demanding meat but Wang has none. Wang's eldest son protests. When Wang tells him about the uncle's membership in the Redbeards, his son suggests that it would be easy to push the uncle and his family into the flood waters. Wang can't commit murder, and besides there would still be the threat of the rest of the bandits. Then the son suggests opium to make harmless addicts of these troublesome relatives.

When the uncle's son lays hands on Wang's younger daughter, Wang realizes he must do something. He persuades Liu to take his future daughter-in-law in. He also buys the opium.

NOTE: Opium trade   Although Europeans did not originally introduce opium into China, the opium trade of the late eighteenth and nineteenth centuries was largely the preserve of the British East India Company, which had a monopoly on the production of Indian opium. The United States picked up and sold the Turkish variety, considered vastly inferior. Although numerous edicts of the Chinese emperors forbidding the opium trade were ignored by both Western and Chinese traders, in 1839 Chinese officials demanded that the traders give up their stores of opium or be refused permission to trade altogether. Giving up the opium for the moment, the British later returned in full naval force in what became known as the First Opium War. The treaty that ended this skirmish in 1842 forced the Chinese to make concessions to foreign trade and open up more areas of China to trade. This enlargement of trading concessions to foreign powers continued and became one of the chief issues in the Boxer movement, whose aim was to throw all foreigners out of China.

CHAPTER 28

Wang casually offers to smoke opium with his uncle but only pretends to smoke. He is careful to keep it away from his own family and from Lotus.

The flood waters recede, and the refugees return and borrow money at high interest rates to rebuild their houses and resume farming. Wang Lung shrewdly insists on the land as security for his loans. He buys land from those who must sell, and his holdings increase. Some sell their daughters, and Wang Lung buys five such slaves in one day. Then comes a man offering a small, thin girl of seven, to whom Lotus takes a fancy. Partly to please Lotus and partly to see the child better fed, he buys this one as well.

The eldest son complains about his cousin who lounges about the house carelessly dressed, peering at the eldest son's young wife as well as the new slaves. He wants his father to move off the farm to the old great house of the Hwangs, leaving behind the parasitical relatives.

At first Wang Lung resists. This old house is his, and the land around it kept them alive through hard times. But then the notion of taking over the mansion of the Hwangs, of whom he was once deathly afraid, appeals to him.

The second son specifies the kind of wife he wants: not a city-bred woman like his brother's wife, who will spend too much money, but a village girl, neither plain nor pretty, a good cook and a thrifty housewife. Wang is amazed at this practical son whom he scarcely knows.

Wang finds half the Hwang mansion rented to poor folk, littered and dirty. Guarding the inner courtyards is an old hag, the pock-marked wife of the former gateman. Wang sits on the raised platform where the Old Mistress sat when she handed over O-lan to him. In a burst of vengeful satisfaction he rents the mansion.

The characters of Wang Lung's two older sons become clear in this chapter, and you may begin to see the personality of the rather silent third son as well. The eldest son resembles his mother physically, with the tall, strongly built frame and ruddy complexion of a northerner, but he dresses and conducts himself with the refined tastes of an aristocrat and scholar, not a humble farmer's son. The second son is shrewd and stingy, with a businessman's concern for money and good management and a practical taste in his choice of a wife. Wang Lung still hopes the third son will love the land, but he merely follows his father across the fields, inattentive and silent.

Which of these boys, if any, do you think will bring happiness to Wang Lung? Although Wang, like most parents, has hopes for his sons, he sees that they have their own ideas. Can you see any reason why they don't want to become farmers? Besides the practical reasons, what kind of an example has Wang shown them?

CHAPTER 29

The mansion is rented. The eldest son and his wife with their possessions and servants, and Lotus and Cuckoo with theirs, move into the once Great House. Wang Lung, however, still can't pull up his roots. He remains with his poor fool, his youngest son, and a farm wife to look after them.

Ching and the farm workers live in the old farm-house, and the uncle, his wife, and son have taken over Lotus' former quarters where they are well out of Wang's sight and hearing. Meanwhile, Ching has found a village bride for Wang's second son.

Ching is old now and Wang will not let him work in the fields, nor does he work there himself. Instead he rents out much of his land to tenant farmers, taking half their crop. However, he still takes pleasure in walking around his fields.

One happy day the uncle's son, bored in a house where there are no longer any women slaves, announces that he is going to the wars. Wang Lung, pretending regret, is generous with silver for the young man's needs and sees him off with relief.

The eldest son's wife is about to give birth. Wang buys incense to burn before the goddess of mercy and promises the goddess a new red robe if his grandchild is a boy. Waiting, he is amazed at the fuss in the house, remembering the stoic calmness with which O-lan bore her children. Lotus, who now has first-wife status, comes with Cuckoo to tell him the child is a boy. Now the pretentious eldest son, in imitation of a great family, has ancestor tablets (a family tree) hung on the wall even though the ancestors were only poor farmers.

Ching is dying. Wang Lung hurries to his old friend's bedside, buys him a fine coffin, and wants to bury him in the family ground, but because Wang's sons object, he has Ching buried just out-side the enclosure. Wang wears mourning clothes and insists that the eldest son do so as well, al-though, as this son says, Ching was only an "up-per servant." Wang Lung feels this loss as though Ching were of his own family. Now at last Wang

Lung, with his retarded daughter and his youngest son, moves into the mansion in the town.

One by one, in this chapter, Wang Lung's links with the past and with the land are finally broken: Ching's death, the renting out of the land, and finally the move to the mansion in town. The eldest son is ashamed of the family's humble beginnings but Wang Lung does not object. He himself has mixed feelings; he is both proud and resentful of his son's refinement. After all, didn't he create his son's attitudes and ambitions? In relationships with parents, isn't their example more important than their speeches? How do you feel when someone preaches one thing and seems to do another?

CHAPTER 30

Wang Lung would like nothing better than to sit in the sun beside his elder daughter and smoke tobacco in his water pipe. But his eldest son pesters him until he gets rid of the poor people who rent the outer sections and lets him refurnish the entire mansion. Then the second son protests at his brother's extravagance in remodeling. Wang Lung, caught between his two sons, promises to put a stop to the spending. The thrifty second son is made steward of the estate, marries his village bride, and moves into the Great House. Meanwhile, Wang's third son also will not be a farmer but wants a tutor.

At long last the uncle dies, and with him the memories of this troublesome family. Wang has his uncle's opium-drugged wife moved into a back section of the mansion with a slave to care for her.

A period of five years passes and Wang Lung

becomes grandfather to four boys and three girls. With a slave nursemaid for each child and slave servants for each of the families, the mansion is a hive of activity. But the eldest and the second sons and their wives have no love for each other, and Wang Lung's only peace is in watching his grandchildren tumbling and playing around him.

The scenes of Wang Lung with two of his sons reveal clearly their fully developed characters. The eldest son is full of pretension and spends money lavishly to show off the family's rise to upper-class status. The second son cares not at all for show but only for money and is even stingy in spending for his own wedding. Although a good steward, he seems likely to become a harsh landlord to the tenant farmers.

Wang is flattered to hear that people in the town now talk of the "great house" of Wang as they used to talk of the House of Hwang. But he warns his eldest son that the family must keep its roots in the soil from which its wealth comes. Now that the youngest son has turned his back on farming as his brothers did, is this very likely? The comparison with the former great house of Hwang leaves little doubt that the new house of Wang will face a similar decline.

CHAPTER 31

Wang Lung has heard of wars being fought, always far away. Suddenly one comes close. A band of soldiers invades the mansion, led by the long absent no-good cousin. In the town the soldiers have broken into every house; when one householder protests, they kill him.

Wang Lung and his sons gather the women and
children into the innermost court and keep it
guarded night and day. But the uncle's son, their
cousin, is a relative and has the run of the house.
He eyes the women, insults the eldest son's wife,
jokes with the bold second daughter-in-law, flat-
ters Lotus, and demands a woman for himself. He
chooses Pear Blossom, the delicate young girl whom
Wang bought at Lotus' request. Lotus orders her
roughly to obey, but the girl weeps in terror and
appeals to Wang Lung, who is touched and decides to spare her. He sends Cuckoo with a more
robust woman to the soldier-cousin who leaves the
woman pregnant, he says, with a grandson for his
opium-drugged mother.

NOTE: Soldiers were a terror to the Chinese
countryside in the 1920s, the period in which the
later part of the novel is set. The central or Nationalist government of the new republic had little
power in the country at large and "war lords"
competed for rule in the provinces. Their private
armies lived off the people, taking their shelter,
food, and women where they pleased and killing
any who dared to cross them. The behavior of the
soldiers in the Wang mansion is a fair example,
and the arrogant, aggressive soldier-cousin gives
a faithful characterization of these men at their
worst.

Little Pear Blossom's appeal could not fail to move
the tenderhearted Wang Lung. Cuckoo, delivering
the substitute woman, observes that the cousin will

pluck whatever fruit is nearest. But you may have caught the hint that Pear Blossom has plans and will be heard from again.

CHAPTER 32

After the soldiers leave, masons and carpenters are called in. The courtyards are cleaned, the garden pools freshened and restocked with goldfish and water lilies, and the flowering trees replanted. The slave woman gives birth to a girl, fortunately for Wang Lung, for as the mother of a son she would have claimed a place in the family. She takes care of the aunt in return for the promise of a husband when the old opium addict dies. Wang Lung keeps the promise and gives the slave to a poor farmer just as the Old Mistress long ago had given O-lan to him. The wheel of fortune has turned full circle, the Wang family has replaced the Hwangs.

The youngest son tells Wang that he wants to join the fighting to free the land of the old system. Wang doesn't understand—he thinks of the land as free because it is his and he can rent it to whomever he chooses. He offers the youth a bride, but the boy dreams of glory and adventure. When he expresses some interest in Pear Blossom, however, Wang Lung denounces him angrily. Something about the little slave affects him strongly. He and his son part in bitterness.

The frictions that are bound to arise in an extended family are well drawn in this chapter. Usually the quarrels among the women of the household are settled with an iron hand by the number-one wife. That would be O-lan's role if she had lived. But you may wonder how even she would have managed with her haughty first daughter-in-law or her sharp-tongued second one, as well as the bad-tempered Lotus.

Wang does not understand his youngest son any better than he did the other two. This boy is aware of the political changes going on in China, and the revolution he talks of is probably the Communist movement that was already forming in China in the 1920s.

CHAPTER 33

Pear Blossom has been in Wang Lung's thoughts. One summer night, sitting alone in his court, he sees her going softly by and calls to her. He reminds her that he is an old man and she is young, but she doesn't mind because old men are kind. So Wang Lung finds a new love in his old age.

Cuckoo notices this new development, and teases Wang Lung, comparing him to the Old Lord before him. He bribes her to break the news to Lotus and buy her whatever presents will keep her quiet. The sons have various reactions. The second son talks of the tenants and says nothing about his father's new concubine. The eldest son seems envious, and Wang suspects he is thinking of a concubine for himself. The youngest son looks fiercely at Pear Blossom and dashes out of his father's court. The next day he is gone for good.

CHAPTER 34

Wang's last flare of passion dies away and his relationship with Pear Blossom becomes one of father to daughter. His one anxiety is for the future of his "poor fool," after he dies. He offers Pear Blossom poison with which to end the helpless creature's life after his own life ends. But Pear Blossom refuses and instead promises to look after his daughter herself.

Lotus has grown enormously fat and spends her time with Cuckoo eating, drinking, and gossiping. Wang goes among his grandchildren, who now number eleven boys and eight girls, but the boys snicker at his ignorance of the new ways and he is discouraged from visiting his sons' quarters. As for his third son, he is said to have become a high official with the revolutionary forces.

With no attachment any longer to the present, Wang moves back into the past, back to the old farmhouse with his retarded daughter, Pear Blossom, and a servant or two. He has chosen his burial place in the family enclosure, and he has his good coffin ready. Pear Blossom tells him that his eldest son has become an official in the town and has taken a second wife, and that his second son is setting up his own grain market.

When these two pay one of their rare visits to their father, he overhears them talking of how they will divide and sell the land. He cries out that they must not sell the land, that it will be the end of the family. They reassure him that they will not, but they smile at one another over his head.

The story of Wang Lung, his family, and his land ends. His sons' wealth is assured. The wealth came from the land but they mean to sell the land. Wang Lung's prediction of the end of the family may well come true, and the saga of a family's rise and fall will be complete. For Wang Lung himself, death is not feared but comes as a promise of rest, and of the peace that he never achieved, except on the land and briefly at the end with Pear Blossom.

NOTE: Pearl Buck continued to describe the fortunes of the House of Wang in two sequels: *Sons* and *A House Divided*. The three sons become, respectively, a decadent landlord, a shady merchant, and a warlord called Wang the Tiger.

A STEP BEYOND

Tests and Answers
TESTS

Test 1

1. Wang's love for Lotus cools when he sees _____ the way she
   A. picks her teeth
   B. squanders her money
   C. treats his retarded daughter

2. When O-lan realizes she is dying, her principal request is _____
   A. to have Wang renounce Lotus
   B. to see her eldest son married
   C. for opium to ease her pain

3. Wang's term of endearment for his first _____ daughter is
   A. "poor fool"   B. "little silkworm"
   C. "sweet plum"

4. Pearl Buck's model for *The Good Earth* was _____
   A. Charles Dickens
   B. Chinese novels
   C. *East Wind, West Wind*

5. Wang's fortunes are determined by _____
   A. his scolding of the earth gods
   B. his stolen treasure as the basis of prosperity
   C. his uncle's membership in the robber gang

6. Wang supplies opium to his uncle to _____

  A. cure the uncle's toothache
  B. give him pleasant dreams
  C. try to make him an addict

7. The eldest son persuades Wang to move _____
   into the Hwang mansion because
   A. he wants finer quarters for his wife
   B. the uncle and his family can be left
      behind
   C. the old farmhouse is too crowded

8. Wang Lung's lifelong, overriding passion _____
   is
   A. the land
   B. his retarded daughter
   C. Lotus Flower

9. The favor Wang asks of his last mistress, _____
   Pear Blossom, is
   A. care for him in his old age
   B. watch over his money for him
   C. poison his retarded daughter when he
      dies

10. Wang works at pulling a riksha in the city _____
    because
    A. he can make more money than in any
       other way
    B. he is too proud to beg
    C. it gives him time to think

11. Why does the Hwang family decline, and how does
    Wang Lung's family appear to be similarly doomed?

12. Compare the roles of wife and concubine in Wang
    Lung's household.

13. What forms of religion does Wang Lung practice
    and which is the most important to him?

14. Compare the relationships between Wang Lung and his two daughters.

15. Describe the circumstances in which O-lan kills her baby. How would you judge her act?

Test 2

1. A Chinese wife's most important function   _____
was to
   A. look after the old parents
   B. bear sons
   C. keep the family together

2. The one act that Wang feels guilty about   _____
toward O-lan is
   A. letting her work in the fields after she has given birth
   B. taking her two small pearls
   C. bringing Lotus Flower into the house

3. The first sign of the declining fortune of the   _____
House of Hwang is the
   A. rude servants
   B. the dusty furniture
   C. the Old Mistress' old coat

4. Pear Blossom wants to become Wang Lung's   _____
concubine because she prefers
   A. old men   B. rich men
   C. widowers

5. Wang Lung's greatest desire in his later   _____
years is for
   A. more grandchildren
   B. a new concubine
   C. peace in his house

6. Wang Lung's youngest daughter cries be-   _____
cause

A. her doll is broken
B. her bound feet hurt
C. she wants a new dress

7. *The Good Earth* is a novel characterized by   _____
   A. flashbacks
   B. complex plotting
   C. straightforward narrative

8. Wang Lung's strongest religious belief is in   _____
   A. the earth gods
   B. the goddess of mercy
   C. ancestor worship

9. In times of stress, Wang Lung's spirits are   _____
   restored by
   A. visiting Lotus Flower
   B. working in his fields
   C. getting drunk

10. Wang Lung switches from riksha pulling   _____
    by day to hauling wagons at night because
    it
    A. pays better
    B. keeps him anonymous
    C. keeps him safe from the soldiers

11. What is the Chinese family attitude toward elders?
    Give positive and negative sides to this tradition.

12. Discuss the practice of foot-binding: its origins, its
    role in the novel, and similarities to other cultural
    practices.

13. Discuss Wang Lung's changing relationship to the
    land as the novel progresses.

14. What evidence does *The Good Earth* give us about
    women's status in traditional China?

15. Wang Lung's fellow worker in the city says: "When the rich are too rich, and when the poor are too poor, there is a way." What does he mean? Give examples to back up your answer.

ANSWERS

Test 1

1. C   2. B   3. A   4. B   5. B   6. C
7. B   8. A   9. C   10. B

11. The Hwang family decline begins when the heirs no longer recognize that the land is the source of their wealth and that it is not inexhaustible. The failing fortunes come across as a kind of moral judgment as well, on the lavish spending for concubines and city pleasures by the young lords and for fashionable weddings and clothes by the daughters. In the Wang family the eldest son has already begun this style of living, and the second son, while watchful with money, is also planning to separate himself from the land as soon as Wang dies. You might draw analogies here if you can, with other countries whose farmers and landowners eventually took their wealth from the land. Have American farmers kept their way of life as their sons have left the land?

12. Confucian teachers wrote that a man took a wife for her virtue and a concubine for her beauty. The women in *The Good Earth* bear out this rule. As a poor farmer's wife, O-lan has duties that include care of the household and of the old father, the preparation of meals, and the sewing and mending of the family's clothes. She also works beside her husband in the fields. But she fulfills the wife's most important function by bearing sons. By contrast, the uncle's wife is as shiftless in her household

duties as he is in farming. But he could not divorce her—supposing he cared enough to do so—because she has borne him a son. Chinese tradition had many causes for divorce, but barrenness, especially the failure to produce a son, was the most important one. A rich man's wife has servants to perform all other duties, but she is obliged to bear sons. As a concubine, Lotus Flower has none of these duties or obligations. She can't perform physical tasks because of her bound feet. In fact, she is not expected to do any work at all, and she is not required to bear children. Her only duty is to make herself a beautiful, desirable object to her master and to be available to him for his pleasure at all times.

13. The three main forms of religion in Wang Lung's village are represented by the Taoist temple, the Buddhist temple, and the temple to the goddess of mercy. On important occasions he makes gifts to all three. In addition, when he comes back with treasure from the southern city, he sets up a picture and candles to the god of riches in his house. In Wang's later years his eldest son installs an ancestor-worship shrine in the family mansion. Wang is pleased that a tablet for his own name is there, even though this is a practice of upper-class rather than peasant families. But Wang Lung's deepest religious feeling is not for these faiths but for two small earthen idols in a field shrine built by his grandfather. It is his belief that this little god and goddess have power over the earth and bring him both his good and his bad fortune. He thanks the idols for good times by burning incense before them, and he scolds them like bad children when drought and famine strike. He also believes in evil spirits that hover in the air and bring trouble down on anyone who boasts of good fortune. Christianity is being taught in China during Wang's time, and

in the southern city a missionary hands out leaflets
showing Christ on the cross. Wang can't read and doesn't
understand the picture, and he gives the leaflet to
O-lan as padding for the soles of the cloth shoes she
makes for the family.

14. Considering the Chinese attitude toward women and
girl children, Wang Lung's relationship with his daughters might almost be called liberated. When his third
child turns out to be a girl, he sees it in the traditional
way as an evil omen (and sure enough, the drought and
famine follow as though to confirm his belief). In Chinese
tradition a daughter had no value. She was only another
mouth to feed until she could be married off at thirteen,
and then her dowry and wedding were still further ex-
penses. Poor families often destroyed a female child at
birth or sold her at an early age as a slave. Even during
the famine, Wang Lung is too tender-hearted to do either.
He knows that O-lan killed the female infant born during the famine, and he does briefly consider her sug-
gestion that they sell their first daughter, also during
the famine. When he realizes later that the girl is retarded, he is horrified by the thought that her masters
would have killed her as a useless slave. His devotion
to his "poor fool" is a touching aspect of his character
but apparently it was not typical in a Chinese family.
After O-lan's death, no one except Wang Lung takes
any responsibility for the girl's care. Wang Lung treats
his younger daughter in a more conventional way, as
an object to advance his status. She is to have her feet
bound so that she can make a good marriage. But here,
too, his soft heart intervenes: he would have her feet
unbound because of the pain. She refuses because, as
O-lan has told her, if she does so, her future husband
will not love her "as you do not love my mother." He

protects this girl's virtue by packing her off to her future home—never to see her again.

15. You can take either side in the case of O-lan's infanticide. Either you believe she was justified by both the custom of her people and the circumstances, or you hold that taking a life is a crime for which there is no possible justification. If the latter is your position, then you must decide what O-lan should have done. She has no milk for this baby, as she herself is starving. She sees that the daughter born the year before is already stunted and near death, and her two small sons are not much better off. In such a situation a mother's only other choice may be to watch her newborn child starve to death.

Test 2
1. B   **2.** B   **3.** C   **4.** A   **5.** C   **6.** B
7. C   **8.** A   **9.** B   **10.** C

11. Other cultures besides the Chinese have made the care of aging parents a family obligation, but with the Chinese it was a binding rule that developed from the teachings of Confucius. A son who offended his father or an elderly relative on his father's side was severely frowned on by the community. When Wang Lung protests to his uncle about the uncontrolled behavior of the uncle's teenage daughter in the town street, the uncle silences him and even extorts money from him by threatening to tell the whole town that Wang was disrespectful to him. Under the pressure of public opinion it is obvious that the elderly would be looked after, although not necessarily with loving care. In the case of Wang's uncle and the uncle's family, the burden is not only heavy but is close to blackmail. You may not approve of how Wang escapes from his obligation, by supplying the uncle and his wife with opium in the hope that they will become addicted (as they do, but that is also their decision, not Wang's). Another obligation this custom lays on Wang is that he must give his old father the first share of whatever food there is during the famine, at the cost of depriving his young children as well as O-lan, who is pregnant. An ideal society might evolve some fairer way of looking after the elderly.

12. According to one of several legends, foot-binding began with a court dancer of the T'ang Dynasty (A.D. 618 to 907) who bound her feet to fit them into tiny dancing shoes. The fashion then spread to all levels of society except the poorest. What pressures would a culture put on women to make them submit to such a crippling custom? You might consider that a court dancer, a concubine, or a prostitute—all of them totally dependent on men's favor—would accept foot-binding. But as you see in *The Good Earth*, the eldest son's wife, who is the daughter of a grain merchant, has bound feet, and O-lan binds her younger daughter's feet so that she may get a good husband. Granted that the girl herself may have no choice in the matter, you also saw that this child would not have her feet unbound, despite the pain, because then her husband "would not love her." A custom that began, as this one apparently did, with royalty, would spread through the population with particular persuasiveness. In China, where very little change occurred over a period of centuries, the custom endured. For a comparison, consider the "wasp" waist of Western fashion in the nineteenth century, which damaged many women's health with its tight corseting but fortunately did not last long. Its purpose, like that of foot-binding, was to please men. Bound feet also added to a man's status, showing that his wife and daughters did not need to do any physical work. How unreasonable of Wang

Lung to be disappointed in O-lan's unbound feet, when as a poor farmer's wife she had to do not only housework but farm work as well!

13. The title, *The Good Earth*, sums up the major theme of both the novel and Wang Lung's life. The land is first of all his livelihood and the source of his prosperity. Money earned in a good harvest, silver extorted from a rich man, O-lan's cache of jewels from a raid, all go to buy land and the seed, the farm animals, and the farm tools to work the land. In the worst of the famine Wang Lung still refuses to sell a single field. The smell of spring in the air, in the southern city where he is a refugee, stirs his longing for the land to a painful intensity. Only once, when O-lan is dying, does he speak of selling the land if it would make her well. She does not let him, for, as she says, she must die some time but the land remains. More than its material value is the spiritual healing that Wang Lung finds in the land, similar to what others find in prayer. Working in rhythm beside O-lan, he forgets the pain of toil. Separation from the land makes him restless and discontented. When he is upset, as when he has quarreled with Lotus over her treatment of his children, a few hours of work in the fields restore his emotional balance. When he moves out of the mansion in town, back to the old farmhouse, it is in order to spend his last years close to the fields that bring him peace of mind.

14. Traditional China was a patriarchal society, that is, a society in which the family head is male and the family name and property are carried on by male heirs. Historically, women in such societies hold an inferior position. Ancient history gives examples of this: in Greece of the Golden Age many women who were not wives became courtesans. Exceptional women still created a place for themselves, for instance the poetess Sappho in Greece. In *The Good Earth* the evidence of women's inferior status accumulates. A woman can be a wife, a concubine, or a prostitute. She can be divorced for not producing sons. A son's birth is celebrated but a daughter's is an evil omen. In the early years of her marriage O-lan appears to have more than a traditional role as a wife. As she advises Wang Lung, and even takes charge at crucial moments, she seems like her husband's equal. But as Wang's fortunes improve, her position declines. It would seem that a woman was allowed to share equally only in poverty and hardship. You may find it interesting to consider which of these inequalities are still true for women in modern times.

15. To Wang Lung and the other famine refugees, the southern city to which they relocate in search of relief is a rich city. It has abundant food in the markets, thriving businesses, and pleasure palaces. Underneath, however, is a layer of poorly paid workers that provide the foundation of the city's wealth. Wang Lung, pulling a riksha or hauling heavy supply wagons in the night, is only one of a large population of the working poor. The gap between rich and poor is enormous, and for the poor there seems to be no hope of escape. Wang's fellow worker, with his statement that "there is a way," seems to be saying that when the gap between rich and poor gets too wide there is bound to be an explosion. Signs of developing unrest do appear, such as street orators and leaflets urging revolution. And indeed there is an explosion—the mob raid that plunders the rich man's house and lifts Wang and his family from destitution to prosperity in a single stroke. You might note that the rich have also seen these signs and have carted their possessions to ships in the river for a hurried escape.

Term Paper Ideas and other Topics for Writing

On the Novel

1. *The Good Earth* has been described as an epic. How would you define this term, and how does the novel qualify for the definition?

2. One of Pearl Buck's achievements was a translation of a Chinese novel, *All Men Are Brothers*. She also wrote on the Chinese novel as a popular literary form aiming purely to entertain. Do you think *The Good Earth*, her most important work, is modeled on the Chinese novel and aims purely to entertain? What do you think the author's aim is in this novel? Support your views with examples.

3. The most severe critics of *The Good Earth* were Chinese intellectuals, many of them emigrants living abroad. They seemed to be embarrassed by the novel's picture of life in China and less acquainted with the farm population and the poor than was Pearl Buck. Do you agree with these critics that the novel gives an unflattering picture of the Chinese people? Make a case for or against such a claim.

4. Pearl Buck says of the neighbors who raid Wang Lung's house during the famine that "they were not bad people except when they were starving." Discuss right and wrong, as illustrated by the way Wang Lung lived his life.

5. The rise of Wang Lung's fortunes and the decline of the House of Hwang are treated as parallels in *The Good*

Earth. Explain this, and discuss what you feel is the author's message in setting up this parallel.

6. During the famine you see that while the people of one region are starving, a city only one hundred miles away has an abundance of food. What were the causes of this unequal distribution of the necessities of life?

7. Echoes sound in the novel of armies marching, battles being fought, robber bands roving the countryside. How are Wang Lung and his family affected by these events? Give some background on what is happening in China during this period.

On Chinese Traditions

1. Describe the traditional obligation to the elderly and its effects on Wang Lung in the novel.

2. Discuss the status of women as illustrated in the novel. Do you see any exceptions to the rule of women's inferiority?

3. Discuss the practice of foot-binding, in the novel and in Chinese tradition, and the relationship of this custom to women's status.

4. What is the place of religion in Wang Lung's life? Where does he place his deepest religious belief? Sketch the peculiarly Chinese blend of religions during the period of the novel.

5. Discuss the difference in relationships of a father with his sons and with his daughters, as seen in the novel.

6. The traditional roles of wife and concubine are contrasted in *The Good Earth*. Discuss these roles in terms of the women in the novel.

Literary Topics

1. Critics have praised Pearl Buck for her drawing of character. Write about any of her characters, contrasting O-lan and Lotus, for example, or Wang's father and the uncle, or Wang's three sons.

2. Describe Wang Lung's character in terms of his strengths, weaknesses, and virtues. Do you note any inconsistencies?

3. Wang Lung's bitterest disappointment is that not one of his three sons cares anything for the land. Discuss his love of the land and why he can't pass on this attachment to his sons.

4. Pearl Buck's writing style in the novel was said to be almost Biblical. Do you agree? Have you a different description of her style? Explain, with examples.

5. Wang Lung's hesitations on the way to the House of Hwang to claim his bride have been described as comic. Are there other moments in the novel that you would consider comic? Can you compare the quality of such comedy with another famous style that combines comedy with pathos?

6. The relationship of Wang with his uncle, the uncle's wife, and the uncle's son is crucial at certain points in the novel. Analyze this relationship, and the ways Wang deals with it.

Social Comment

1. Why does the Hwang family fail, and how is Wang Lung's family similarly doomed? Discuss the question of landed wealth. Can you make a comparison between China's farm society as shown in this novel, and other farm-based cultures?

2. Pearl Buck gives a detailed picture of the city and its contrast between rich and poor. Discuss this contrast and its implications for political change.

3. An aspect of Chinese architecture is the way additions are made to a house as the household grows and needs more space: for example, how Wang Lung provides an "apartment" for Lotus Flower. Describe the structure and its advantages for an extended family.

4. As Wang Lung prospers, he changes his style of life and dress. Beginning with cutting off his queue, describe the step-by-step changes in Wang Lung from his first visit to Lotus Flower in the House of Flowers.

Further Reading
CRITICISM AND BIOGRAPHY

Doyle, Paul A. *Pearl S. Buck.* Boston: Twayne Publishers, 1980. A critical biography.

Harris, Theodore F. *Pearl S. Buck: A Biography.* New York: John Day Co., 1969. Written during Mrs. Buck's lifetime and with her collaboration.

Litz, A. Walton, ed. *American Writers,* Supplement II, Part 1. New York: Charles Scribner's Sons, 1981.

Spencer, Caroline (pseudonym for Grace Sydenstricker Yaukey). *The Exile's Daughter.* New York: Coward McCann, 1944. A highly personal biography dealing with Pearl Buck's parents and the first half of Mrs. Buck's life, written by her sister.

Spiller, Robert E., et al. *A Literary History of the United States.* New York: Macmillan, 1960.

Stirling, Nora. *Pearl Buck: A Woman in Conflict.* Piscataway, New Jersey: New Century, 1983.

Wagenknecht, Edward. *Cavalcade of the American Novel*. New York: Henry Holt and Co., 1952.

AUTHOR'S OTHER WORKS
(SELECTED)

Novels

East Wind, West Wind. New York: John Day Co., 1930. The impact of Western ways on two young couples, one a Chinese physician and his tradition-minded wife, the other this wife's brother educated in the United States and his American wife whom he brings back to China.

Sons. New York: John Day Co., 1932. First sequel to *The Good Earth*, telling the further story of Wang Lung's three sons: one a decadent landlord, another a shady merchant, and the third a warlord called Wang the Tiger.

The Mother. New York: John Day Co., 1934. A young Chinese farm wife, deserted by her husband, brings up her children alone.

A House Divided. New York: Reynal and Hitchcock, 1935. The warlord's son Yuan seeks his roots on his grandfather's old farm, in America, and back in the "new" China. Second sequel to *The Good Earth*.

This Proud Heart. New York: Reynal and Hitchcock, 1938. Buck's first significant novel with an American setting. It is the story of a sculptor struggling to combine marriage, children, and her work as an artist. Perhaps a reflection of Buck's own effort to find self-realization as a writer.

The Patriot. New York: John Day Co., 1939. China and Japan in the years 1920 to 1940.

Dragon Seed. New York: John Day Co., 1942. Realistic portrayal of the Japanese invasion of China coupled

with a romantic love story. Enjoyed popular success
both as book and motion picture.

The Promise. New York: John Day Co., 1943. A war novel
of the disastrous British-Chinese campaign in Burma.

The Townsman. New York: John Day Co., 1945. The first
of five novels under the pseudonym of John Sedges.
An American "Western," with a schoolteacher instead of a gunfighter as its hero.

Pavilion of Women. New York: John Day Co., 1946. The
heroine is a brilliant Chinese woman influenced by a
heretical but deeply humanitarian priest.

Kinfolk. New York: John Day Co., 1949. The story of an
American-trained Chinese physician who works among
farmers. The background is the rise of Communism
in China.

Short Story Collections

The First Wife and Other Stories. New York: John Day Co.,
1933.

Fourteen Stories. New York: John Day Co., 1961.

The Good Deed and Other Stories of Asia, Past and Present.
New York: John Day Co., 1969.

Biography and Autobiography

The Exile. New York: Reynal and Hitchcock, 1936. Buck's
biography of her mother.

Fighting Angel. New York: Reynal and Hitchcock, 1936.
Buck's biography of her father.

The Child Who Never Grew. New York: John Day Co.,
1950. The story of Buck's retarded daughter.

My Several Worlds. New York: John Day Co., 1954. Autobiography.

A Bridge for Passing. New York: John Day Co., 1962.
Autobiography.

Other Nonfiction
The Chinese Novel. New York: John Day Co., 1939.
The People of Japan. New York: Simon and Schuster, 1966.
China As I See It. Ed. by Theodore F. Harris. New York: John Day Co., 1970.
China Past and Present. New York: John Day Co., 1972.

Translation
All Men Are Brothers. New York: John Day Co., 1937. Picaresque novel of a robber band.

Glossary

Ancestor worship   Worship of earlier heads of the family in a household shrine consisting of tablets bearing their names.

Anhwei (Anhui)   East central province of China, in the northern part of which Pearl Buck spent four years with her missionary husband. The setting of *The Good Earth*.

Buddhism   Religion of "enlightenment" founded by India's great religious teacher, called Buddha (sixth century B.C.), and brought to China in the first century A.D. by Indian priests.

Ching Dynasty   China's last imperial dynasty, 1644–1911; also called Manchu Dynasty.

Confucius   China's great philosopher and teacher, 551–478 B.C.

Geomancer   A folk prophet who reads the future by the patterns of a handful of earth thrown on the ground.

Kiangsu (Jiangsu)   A province on the east coast, east of Anhui and north of Shanghai.

Riksha, also **jinriksha** or **jinrikisha** A two-wheeled carriage with shafts for a human puller.

Taoism The third of China's three major religions, founded on the teachings of the philosopher Lao-tse (sixth century B.C.).

Warlord Provincial dictator in China in the period of *The Good Earth*. Ruled his region by means of a private army.

The Critics

A Historical View

Ernest Hemingway discovered a brotherhood between the American and the Spanish rebel, and Pearl Buck a link between the Yankee and the Chinese— the brotherhood of democracy. [She was part of] the "little Renaissance" of American literature, a flowering of writers from all corners of the United States in a search for values and control of forms. . . . [Buck was one of] the American writers that spread the 20th century recognition of American literature abroad . . . in books distinguished by scope, human warmth, reasonableness . . . [*The Good Earth* was published in three translations in China, one of them cut and garbled.] The other two were widely discussed in the Chinese press, where some of the reviewers—a minority, as might be expected— thought that Mrs. Buck presented a true picture.

—*A Literary History of the United States*, 1960

A Chinese Attack

Since Mrs. Buck does not understand the meaning of the Confucian separation of man's kingdom from that of woman, she is like someone trying to write a story of the European Middle Ages without understanding the rudiments of chivalric standards and the institution of Christianity. None of her major

descriptions is correct except in minor details. . . .
Its implied comparison between Western and Eastern ways is unjust to the latter.

> —Younghill Kang in *The New
> Republic*, 1931

An American Defense

Mrs. Buck has enabled us to witness and appreciate
the patience, frugality, industry, and indomitable
good humor of a suffering people, whose homes
the governing intellectuals would hide from the sight
of the world.

> —editorial in *The New York Times*,
> 1931

On Style and Characterization

The style of *The Good Earth* is one of its most appealing qualities. It derives from the mellifluous prose
of the King James Version of the Bible intermingled
with the technique of the traditional Chinese sagas.
In many respects the two style sources are similar.
The choice of words is clear, simple, and vivid, and
features considerable use of parallelism and bal-
anced sentence structure. . . . There is an archaic
flavoring derived from the choice of words, the rep-
etition, and the natural musical flow of the parallelism. . . . The style is expertly tuned to the subject
matter—simple but forceful, moving but stoic,
graceful but never excessive. . . . Her characters are
not overwhelmed in a deterministic world, op-
pressed by the forces of heredity and environment.
They realize that through the exercise of choices,
through hard work and human initiative, difficulties and problems can be overcome and despair sub-
dued. . . . *The Good Earth* possesses an affirmative
belief in human nature.

> —*American Writers*, Supplement II,
> Part 1, 1981

The Foremost Interpreter

She is the foremost interpreter in fiction of Chinese
life; she thinks her novels about China in Chinese,

and what has been called their Biblical style is really
a Chinese style. Sometimes she shocks Western
readers by describing Chinese customs from the
Chinese point of view, not feeling it necessary to
violate the integrity of her work by breaking in upon
it to announce that she personally does not approve
of what is taking place. . . . She never wanted to
write about the Chinese as such; she wanted to write
about people; the people she knew best just hap-
pened to be Chinese.

— Edward Wagenknecht, *Cavalcade
of the American Novel*, 1952

Buck's Achievement

Although she has been ignored by many critics and
not accepted by the literary establishment, it may
be maintained that she has written at least three
books of undoubted significance: *The Good Earth* and
the biographies of her father and mother. Certainly,
The Good Earth is a masterpiece that will be remem-
bered by subsequent generations as a work that
powerfully and movingly describes a whole way of
life. . . . Her books offer thoughtful and provocative
insights into some of the most challenging issues
mankind has faced and continues to face. It is this
quality, generally overlooked by critics, that gives
value to her later work.

— Paul A. Doyle, *Pearl S. Buck*,
1980

NOTES

NOTES

NOTES

NOTES

NOTES

NOTES